UNIVERSITY OF
WOLVERHAMPTON

Feminist Perspectives on Language

FEMINIST PERSPECTIVES SERIES

Series Editors:

Professor Pamela Abbott, University of Teesside
Professor Claire Wallace, Institute for Advanced Studies, Austria
and University of Derby, UK

FEMINIST PERSPECTIVES SERIES

Feminist Perspectives on Language

Margaret Gibbon

LONGMAN
London and New York

Pearson Education Limited
Edinburgh Gate
Harlow
Essex CM20 2JE
England
and Associated Companies throughout the world

*Published in the United States of America
by Pearson Education Inc., New York*

*Visit us on the World Wide Web at:
http://www.awl-he.com*

© Pearson Education Limited 1999

First published 1999

ISBN 0 582 35636 9

British Library Cataloguing-in-Publication Data

A catalogue record for this book is available from the British Library

Library of Congress Cataloging-in-Publication Data

Gibbon, Margaret.
   Feminist perspectives on language / Margaret Gibbon.
      p.   cm. — (Feminist perspectives series)
   Includes bibliographical references (p.) and index.
   ISBN 0–582–35636–9
   1. Language and languages—Sex differences.   2. Sexism in
language.   3. Feminism.   I. Title.   II. Series.
P120.S48G53   1999
306.44—dc21   98–47350
                                                                      CIP

Typeset by 35 in 10/12pt New Baskerville
Produced by Addison Wesley Longman Singapore (Pte) Ltd.,
Printed in Singapore

Contents

Series editors' preface

The aim of the Feminist Perspectives series is to provide a concise introduction to different topics from a feminist perspective. The topics were chosen as being of interest for students on a range of different degree courses and in a range of different disciplines. They reflect the current interest in feminist issues and in women's studies in a wide range of fields. The series aims to provide a guide through the burgeoning and sometimes rather arcane literatures which have grown around various feminist topics. The texts are written by experienced teachers and academics providing lively and interesting accounts of topics of current interest. They include examples and case studies or statistical information where relevant in order to make the material more accessible and stimulating. The texts contain chapter outlines and summaries for convenient, quick access. There are also suggestions for further reading.

We are pleased to be able to present to our readers the first book in the series, the book by Margaret Gibbon, *Feminist Perspectives on Language*. As editors, we found this book a real pleasure to read and it provides a suitable flagship for the launch of the series. Margaret Gibbon starts by considering whether men and women speak a different language, a subject which is often discussed in the popular press. She then goes on to cover the main theories of language use from a feminist perspective as well as feminist theories of language, giving us a clear, critical overview. She considers if we speak the language or if the language speaks us and other philosophical and linguistic problems in a down to earth and often witty way. The book touches upon problems not just in linguistics but also in sociology, social psychology, literature and many other disciplines. After all, we all use language. This book is not just an

informative text for those who want some introduction to the subject matter – it is also an excellent and entertaining read. We hope
it brings you also to new insights in a pleasurable way.

Claire Wallace and Pamela Abbott

Acknowledgements

I welcome this opportunity to express my gratitude to the many people who helped me endure the relatively lonely process of writing this book. At the School of Applied Language and Intercultural Studies of Dublin City University, I'd like to thank Jenny Williams who has encouraged all my undertakings, Heinz Lechleiter for drawing my attention to the political significance of metaphor and Catherine O'Riordan for being a walking encyclopaedia of linguistics. I'm also deeply indebted to Jennifer Pearson for her excellent example and Lynne Bowker for her unfailing interest in the project. Most especially, I want to thank Helen O'Meara for her infectious enthusiasm for all things linguistic, as well as the best of friendship.

I thank Irish taxpayers and Dublin City University for help with secretarial expenses and Brenda O'Mara for expert skills in preparing the manuscript. Other university colleagues contributed their expertise: Jane Fahy's technical wizardry and David O'Callaghan's photographic know-how are much appreciated. Thanks are also due to Deirdre Beecher and Edel O'Brien and their colleagues at the library, as well as to Celine Jameson who took the trouble to arrange my teaching hours to leave me blocks of time for research.

I also wish to record my appreciation of students and friends with whom I discussed many of the ideas developed in the book: Liz Ryan-Larragy, Tom Clonan, Alison Gourvès-Hayward, Sharon Brady and Ann Meehan all encouraged me in different ways and I found their commitment to their own work quite inspiring. I thank my friend Patricia Wallace for the many walks we took together to take a break from our respective projects.

Words fail me to express my heartfelt thanks to Sami Moukaddem.

My Welsh family, especially my parents, gave me moral support, and my Irish family sustained me throughout this enterprise, not least by keeping me fed and watered and by never complaining about my long and frequent stints at the desk. I also really appreciated the light relief provided by hours of meal-time banter and repartee, starring Sheila, John, Ruth, Nadine, Jay-Jay, Clare and Davey. This book is dedicated to them.

Margaret Gibbon

The publishers are grateful to News International for permission to reproduce a headline from *The Sun* newspaper (20.12.86). We have been unable to trace the copyright holder in the poem 'Vagina Sonnet' by Joan Larkin and would appreciate any information that would enable us to do so.

Chapter 1

Introduction

Chapter outline

This chapter has the following aims:

- to introduce the general aims of the book as a whole
- to introduce four different strands of feminism and the views of language associated with them
- to provide an outline of the remainder of the book

Aims of this book

This book, written for students of women's studies, linguistics, communications and media studies as well as the interested lay reader, aims to provide an up-to-date account of developments in research focusing upon the interaction of language and **gender**. Such research, conducted since the early 1970s, ranges over many themes and draws on a number of disciplines. Moreover, as the title of the book suggests, there is not one but several perspectives on language within **feminism**. The book aims to provide a short and accessible introduction to the topic and to provide guidance for further reading for those interested in pursuing any of the lines of enquiry outlined in it.

One of my reasons for writing the book was my own uneasy feeling about the growing popularity of books telling couples, but especially heterosexual women, how to save their marriage by tuning in to the different talking styles of women and men. I felt strongly that if communication styles were different (and I wasn't convinced of that), they were also unequal. Also, I felt that language did not play such an important role in relationships. Surely other problems explained marital disharmony: arguments about sharing of responsibility for housework and childcare, control of money, access to space and leisure, sexual difficulties, unemployment, alcoholism, violence, and many other issues seemed to figure far more than language in the conversations I enjoyed with married women friends. Focusing on communication styles seemed to me a way of avoiding the bigger issues of inequality in heterosexual relationships and in society in general. Even if, in researching the popular and academic literature on women's and men's conversational styles, I were to find proof of such differences, I would want to know how they come about, how they are acquired and who benefits or whose aims are served by having women and men talking at cross purposes. Thus, one of the aims of the book became the investigation of sex-difference research and its popularization, along with the desire to understand why feminists look for sex differences in linguistic behaviour at all.

Feminists in the 1970s and 1980s had fine-tuned theories of gender to show how arbitrary and constructed most differences are between women and men. Surely looking for sex differences in language use could only contribute to society's common sense and erroneous views that women and men were just different, the basic belief underlying male domination. This system depends on reifying female–male difference and naturalizing the gendered social arrangements we come to take for granted. Why would feminists, of all people, begin research by asking 'What are the differences between women and men?' as opposed to 'Are there differences between women and men?' or 'How do women use language to signal womanliness as defined by our culture? How do men use language to signal manliness?'

My uneasiness with the formulation of research topics means that I have foregrounded questions of methodology and interpretation in Part II of this book, which deals with language in use, communication styles and the analysis of conversation. Despite reservations about sex-difference research models, I have attempted to present the findings of such research as thoroughly and as fairly as research from the two main competing positions: the dominance paradigm, which focuses on inequality and power rather than difference, and the postmodernist perspective, which attempts to highlight the malleability of gender and thus challenge the dichotomy underlying both difference and dominance perspectives.

The aims of Part I of the book are quite different. Rather than asking questions about users of language, their behaviour, patterns of conversational interaction and so on, the first part of the book looks at language itself. We learn a language without difficulty normally – at least our first or native tongue. The dominant linguistic model argues that humans are, from birth, 'wired' for language. We tend to take language for granted and, despite frequent misunderstandings, slips of the tongue and unsuccessful attempts at communication, generally think of language as a simple tool we use to share information and express feelings and ideas. Or as a vehicle. Our usual metaphors for language tend to refer to everyday objects we can use and control. Metaphor is always significant. We are supposedly 'wired' for language. This metaphor views the human being, or the brain, as an electronic circuit board, an updating of a 500-year-old view of the human being as a machine. Language is a 'tool' or 'vehicle'. We use tools to do what we want; we control them. We drive vehicles; we control them.

But what if language controlled us? What if, rather than being a vehicle we could drive wherever we wanted to go, which served us and our needs, language turned out to be a prison which limited our capacity for vision, movement, innovative thinking, imagination? Does language set us free or trap us? Does our language affect how we come to understand the world around us? Is our language sexist? If so, does that reflect male dominance in society? Is language a mirror? Or does sexist language somehow help to create sexism?

Feminists seek to change society in radical ways. To do this, we need to understand how it works, to identify sites where we can intervene to make changes. Most human interaction involves language in some way: to fail to teach a child to speak, to listen, to interact verbally with others would constitute severe neglect. We are the talking animal. Language is so central, so fundamental to social interaction, to our becoming who we are that no one interested in influencing and inflecting their society can ignore it.

Part I of this book introduces theories about language, about the relationship of language to culture and society and about how women and men are spoken of in language, in this case in English. Its primary aim is to raise awareness of language and its intricacies, to share the sense of awe it inspires in me.

Feminisms and language

Feminism is, as well as a practice, a philosophy which challenges social arrangements regarding women's and men's relative value, status, positions, roles and opportunities. There is not a single, unified body of feminist thought. On the contrary, feminists differ in what they focus on as central to women's social oppression in the present and in their views of the ultimate cause of women's exploitation, marginalization and devaluing in society. Making sense of the wide range of views, positions and counter positions can be difficult, and when we try to categorize feminists we tend to force a structure on what may better be viewed as a nebulous movement. Nevertheless, I will propose just such a schema, dividing feminists into four main groupings, each corresponding to a particular view of language. In drawing up this typology, I am more than aware that the positions within it overlap, and that many feminists support language proposals from other feminist groupings whose views they may not share on other issues. Feminists who do not believe that language reform can work, do nonetheless reform their own language and encourage others to do so, to give a simple example. Other views, however, can engender enormous resistance from opposed groups.

Liberal feminism

Detractors of liberal feminism, such as radical and socialist feminists, argue that it 'changes the women not the world'. Rooted in eighteenth-century liberal philosophy, this type of feminism views the women's struggle as one of equal rights with men. Noting that men enjoyed rights denied to women, early feminists fought for the right to vote and be elected to political office; to own, transmit and inherit property in their own name; for equal access to education at all levels; for employment opportunities equal to men's; and for custody of their own children. The struggle is not over – the Equal Rights Amendment has yet to be ratified in the USA for example – but this movement does have many successes to its credit. In most Western countries today, girls as well as boys are educated, women may engage in employment without a husband's permission, may exercise their right to vote, stand for office, lead a trade union or political party or occupy the country's top position as head of state. Discrimination against women does, however, continue in many forms, making women's access to such arenas more difficult. Nonetheless, in most cases, legal prohibitions have been lifted, making women formally equal to men. But which men? Men are not equal among themselves, but divided by class, race, ethnicity, sexuality and so on. To which men do liberal feminists aim to be equal? Who aspires to university education when the majority of the population, **female** and male, are barely literate? Liberal feminism is taxed with being a white, upper- or upper-middle-class movement which serves the aspirations of a minority of privileged women. In practice, however, many of the gains achieved by such women have benefited other women too.

Women of liberal feminist persuasion tend to be active in publicly funded institutions, educational bodies, legal professions, politics and business. The business community, along with educationalists, developed assertiveness-training for women in the early 1980s. This very successful initiative targeted heterosexual women, especially, but not only, women in paid employment, and ran courses for them on effective language skills. Beneath their philosophy a deficiency model of women's language operated: women had been conditioned to speak deferentially and to avoid verbal conflict. The workplace required more forceful speech. Therefore, to be effective in the workplace where men's speech norms prevailed, women needed to be re-trained. This movement is discussed in Chapters 5 and 7.

Involved as they were in promoting employment equality for women, liberal feminists also focused on language reform, specifically the re-naming of job titles. As traditional male strongholds began to admit women following employment equality legislation in the early 1970s, new names were needed for women occupying jobs named for male incumbents: *lady salesman* would not do. Language reform is discussed in Chapter 4. While many feminists have been critical of assertiveness training (Crawford 1995 offers an excellent critique), language reform has enjoyed more general support. Debates about it tend to focus not on the principle of inclusive language, but on the rationale for it, or the view of language and its relationship to thought, perception and reality. This is discussed in Chapter 3.

Materialist feminism

Unlike liberal feminism, which focuses upon psychology, 'conditioning', social roles, and rights to explain women's condition in society, materialist feminism is based on an examination of material forces, specifically the economic underpinnings of discrimination. Materialist feminists argue that women's oppression is at root, economic. A central focus is the gender division of labour within the workplace and in the family and the social and cultural arrangements and beliefs which uphold it. The relationship between class and gender, between socialism and feminism, was of central concern to feminists of this persuasion throughout the early and mid-1980s (Barrett 1988). This movement was particularly well developed in Britain. A French variant (Delphy 1984, Delphy and Leonard 1992) differed from British materialist feminism in arguing the primacy of the division of labour within the home, over that in paid employment, and by claiming that women formed a class in opposition to the class of men on the basis of this 'domestic mode of production'.

Neither the British nor the French groupings focused specifically on language in their own writings. However, those working within the Marxist tradition did pay great attention to ideology and cultural support for capitalism. Indeed, attention to culture increased in the late 1980s to dominate debates throughout the 1990s. While adopting language reformists' suggestions in their own speech, most materialists argued that changing the language would not change the material conditions underlying class or gender oppression. In France, a bigger battle faced Delphy and her associates: the emergence to prominence of a radically different feminist grouping, Psychanalyse et Politique, whose views on language and its relation to gender were diametrically opposed to their own. French materialist feminists such as Delphy and Guillaumin were drawn into a debate on language in response to the writings of feminists associated with the Psychanalyse et Politique group (Duchen 1986, 1987, Guillaumin 1987, Delphy 1984, Leclerc 1974, Marks and De Courtivron 1981). This group was arguing for a distinctive woman's language (parole de femme, parler femme) based upon woman's experience of her body. For Delphy, there could be no experience of the body unmediated by the social construction of ourselves as gendered beings. The 'meaning' of a bodily experience such as menstruation, childbirth or lactation is not given by our body, but by a society in which discrimination against women is axiomatic. Material conditions, not ideas, determine how we experience events like menstruation, she argued.

Concern with ideology and the linkage between class, gender and other oppressive and exploitative social divisions led socialist

feminists into critical linguistics, a branch of linguistics which examines texts to identify how social relations are inscribed in them.
Recent feminist stylistics draws on such an approach to text (Mills
1995). However, a shift from a focus on written language to spoken
language means that currently, the most well-known and publicly
discussed views of language are those of cultural feminists.

Cultural feminism

In the 1980s a radical shift occurred in feminism. Analyses focusing on women's subordinate status and on their oppression by men
gave way to a current of feminism which celebrates women's differences from men. Where liberal feminists had argued to give
women rights to make them equal to (and more like) men, and
materialists had shown how difference really meant inequality,
cultural feminists focused on re-evaluating women's particular way
of being in the world. This radical feminist grouping viewed women
as fundamentally different from men and aimed to have this difference celebrated. Rather than seeking to make women like men,
they aimed to show that women's ways were valuable and not to be
given up. Indeed, many argued that women were morally superior
to men (Daly 1978, Gilligan 1982). 'Women's language', once viewed
as deficient, weak and ineffective, was now celebrated as the vehicle
for women's experience, identity, values and meanings. Among
linguists, research on cross-sex conversation, which showed how men
dominated women verbally, gave way to research on all-female
groups or to comparisons of girls' and boys' speech at play or in
laboratory settings. This work is reviewed in Part II, Chapter 6.

In France, cultural feminism took a different slant, focused as it
was on psychoanalysis and women's writing. Whereas American
cultural feminists in the main accepted that it was socialization
which led to the emergence of a female sub-culture with its own
norms and values, French advocates of the Psychanalyse et Politique
perspective rooted their analysis in a feminist reworking of Freudian psychoanalysis, or rather of a form of psychoanalysis developed
by French analyst and theoretician Jacques Lacan. It would be
impossible to do justice to their theoretical positions in an introductory text such as this. Further reading is recommended for those
who would like to follow up the brief outline provided here (see
Cameron 1985, Chapter 7 for an introduction).

This tendency, Psychanalyse et Politique, often erroneously called
'French feminism' as if other positions did not exist, has made

language and writing absolutely central to their concerns. Arguing that other feminisms reinforce patriarchy by aiming to make women equal to (the same as) men, Psychanalyse et Politique focuses on how women become women, that is, viewed as the negative or absent reflection of men. As we enter the Symbolic (culture mediated by language), women have to take up a position in the way defined by a male-dominated understanding of reality. Rather than being recognized as herself, different and unique, woman is viewed as a lack or an absence. This is traced to the primacy of the phallus in Freudian analysis. According to the theory, when children view and compare their genitals with those of the other sex, boys are seen to have a penis, girls to lack one, leading to the castration complex. Feminist re-visioning of this event argues that it is inappropriate to imagine women's genitals as an absence or lack. French feminists argue that women's sexual organs are plural and at root make woman complete and auto-erotic (Irigaray 1977, translated 1985). According to theorists in this movement, the plurality of sources of pleasure in the female body is reflected in women's consciousness, identity and language. Writings from women in this movement typically employ loose syntax, unfinished sentences, words spelled and respelled to suggest alternate, plural readings and other devices to suggest openness or lack of fixity and closure. The translation of such texts is not without problems, as puns and respellings do not pass easily into other languages. Feminists in translation studies have argued that Irigaray's and Cixous' transatlantic passage was more than choppy (Simon 1996, von Flotow 1997). Nevertheless, for many feminist academics in American universities, this form of feminism *is* French feminism. Ironically perhaps, it is better known outside France than in France, albeit often misinterpreted. Detractors point to the elitism associated with its more arcane texts, to the cost of psychoanalysis, its alleged misogyny and to the politics of a group who used the law to patent the name 'women's liberation movement' to prevent other groups from using it. Their views on language reform are discussed briefly in Chapter 4.

American cultural feminists' concern with the body has been more political, focusing on compulsory heterosexuality, rape, pornography and trafficking in women. Their proposals for language reform involved renaming of women's experiences and those of other oppressed minorities, giving rise to what became known as **politically correct** language. This is discussed in Chapter 4.

Postmodernist feminism

I'll never forget the frissons of pleasure I experienced one day as I watched a TV chat show in which a Black woman (I think it was Maya Angelou) quizzed a Conservative party man about his use of the words 'Black people'. 'Do you mean coffee-coloured, caffe latte, brown, plum, aubergine, blue-black or what?' she asked him. Or words to that effect. Neither my memory nor my word-power could do justice to her magnificent question, which split his black–white dichotomy to smithereens. Our language makes racial categories seem to exist in the real world, whereas there actually is not any set of biological criteria available to define race (Omi and Winant 1994). Given all the possible mixtures, skin colour is not a dichotomy as the Conservative spokesperson supposed, but a continuum. Yet our language fails to reflect this adequately, and the few terms which do exist carry negative connotations: *métis, half-caste, mulatto, coloured*. I would argue that their negative connotations even outrank those of *Black* in white racist society. They challenge the white–black polarization and remind us there is one race, the human race. Could it be the same for sex? Bing and Bergvall argue that it is:

> Because the terms *female* and *male* insufficiently categorise our experience, English also includes *tomboy, sissy, bisexual, gay, lesbian, hermaphrodite, androgyne, transvestite, transsexual, transgendered individual*, etc.
>
> (1996: 2)

Postmodernists focus on how our language creates the categories and identities we come to see as natural, including sex and gender. Our society denies the very existence of inter-sexed individuals; any infant born with ambiguous sex organs or a mis-match between genital and chromosomal sex is made into a girl or boy by surgery or drugs or both. Adult transsexuals convince medics at 'gender dysphoria' clinics that they have been born 'into the wrong body' in order to qualify for medical mutilation (Raymond 1979). Following surgery, male-to-constructed female transsexuals are taught how to speak, walk, dress, act, make-up and sit (ibid: 94). Clearly changing one's genitals by surgery is insufficient to pass as a woman: gender is learned.

Materialist feminists like Delphy also argue that gender is socially constructed and prescribed. However, whereas materialists consider that our identity becomes gendered by material practices and thereafter remains relatively stable, postmodernists argue that language itself is responsible for our gendering and that we perform our gender repeatedly day after day in ways prescribed by our culture. Gender, to postmodernists, is not a dichotomy but a continuum: we can present ourselves to the world as more or less feminine or masculine, as more or less heterosexual, as more or less passive, active, deferential, authoritative. When being 'emotional' is part of a feminine stereotype, women may enact masculinity by adopting a non-emotional persona, performing authority counter to role prescriptions (McElhinny 1998). People may use language, body posturing, dress and sexual practices to enact a transgendered identity (Butler 1990, Devor 1989, Epstein and Straub 1991, Garber 1991 cited in McElhinny 1998). According to Butler, if our gendered identity comes to feel stable and to appear to pre-exist our enactments of, say, a feminine self, this is due to 'a regulated process of repetition' (1990: 145). Our agency, or ability to act beyond prescription, can be read from our capacity to subvert the script, to make variations on the repetition. For her, there is no doer before the deed: the deed (speech, dress, sexual performance) creates the doer. The parody of feminine behaviour performed by male transvestites draws attention to how all gender performance *is* a performance, an act rather than a natural extension of our anatomical inheritance. Linguists focusing on discourse have begun to use postmodernist views on performativity of gender to analyze conversational practice. Arguing against earlier interpretations of gender as a given polarity McElhinny writes:

> I also, however, focus on these similarities between the interactional styles of female and male police officers as a response to the extant literature on language and gender, which often begins by asking what the differences between men's and women's language are, and which, in its focus on women versus men, threatens to reify social differences in ways not so very different from sex-based essentialist theories. I argue here for a more flexible definition of gender and its effects on language use, one that accords the speaker more agency to develop a speaking style based upon their occupational choices, personal histories, sexuality, lifestyles, and more.
>
> (1998: 322)

This issue, the performativity of gender by language practices, is discussed briefly in Chapter 6.

This short overview of feminist positions on language aimed to help the reader make sense of the debates which are presented in greater detail in the remaining chapters. There is no accepted terminology for the feminist groups outlined; in linguistics, three general positions are recognized. These are the dominance approach (largely corresponding to materialist feminism's concern with exploitation and control); the difference approach (corresponding to cultural feminism); and the postmodernist approach. Faced with the same experiment and the same data or findings, feminists from each of these perspectives may come to three different interpretations. Chapters 5 and 6 develop arguments to account for this.

While this may appear confusing for the reader new to this subject, it is important to recognize that most progress in a discipline occurs in a climate of debate, not when orthodoxy reigns. Early work on interruption in conversation by linguists working in the dominance framework found men interrupted women far more than the reverse (Zimmerman and West 1975). Dissatisfaction with the findings, the approach and the methodology led difference approach linguists to develop our understanding of interruption so that it is now seen as having more than one function and can be interpreted as a signal of involvement (Coates 1996). This approach has, in its turn, been questioned by those with a postmodernist perspective, who show that a focus on difference obscures similarity and overlap as well as other variables acting in the research environment (Freed and Greenwood 1996). This simple example shows how healthy such debate is to an emerging field of study.

Outline of remaining chapters

The book is divided into two separate parts, corresponding to linguists' conventional division: language as system and language in use. In the first part, the aim is to interrogate language to see if language reflects the social arrangements of society with regard to gender. Is language sexist? Can it be changed? How does language affect thought? Can language-reform work? These are some of the questions Part I will address, by reviewing and discussing available research written from a variety of feminist perspectives.

Chapter 2 introduces key terms and ideas used by theorists exploring language as system. When we talk or write about chemistry or biology, we need a special vocabulary; the same is true of language study. Most people learn their native language without ever needing the special vocabulary linguists use to describe language. They may encounter this **metalanguage** as teenagers or adults in a formal setting. We cannot avoid encountering these terms in reading what feminists and others have come to understand about the connections between language and gender. This chapter will discuss various views of language as simply as possible and explain technical terms by using examples, illustrations and quotations. Readers are also referred to the glossary at the end of the book. Where necessary, comparisons with other languages will be made, although generally the focus is on English.

Chapter 3 explores the relationship between language, thought and reality. Those who favour language reform clearly believe that it makes a difference whether we use *he, he or she* or *they* to refer to a person of unspecified sex. Does using *he* in such cases constitute a sexist practice? Does it matter? Is it just a rule? Do people think of women when *he* is used in this way? In other words, does language reflect social reality straightforwardly, does it reinforce our social reality and its gendered nature, or does language even create our reality in some way, by affecting how we perceive and interpret it? Many feminists believe language does affect our perception, and base their views on an idea known as linguistic relativity, first mooted to explain cultural differences between white anthropologists and the peoples they studied. The chapter presents arguments for and against linguistic relativity and includes an exercise to raise awareness about cultural difference.

Chapter 4, which ends Part I, examines in detail most of the main issues raised by feminists who have sought changes to the English language. How is gender marked in English? How does the language 'talk about' women and men? What do swear words and insults tell us about society's views of women? By looking at the names we give children, at politically correct language, at job-titles and forms of address among others, this chapter will investigate whether English is a sexist language or if it depends on the way it is used by speakers and writers. Which leads us to Part II, language in use.

Chapter 5 introduces the second part of the book, 'Language in use'. A variety of feminist perspectives exist on the issue of women's and men's use of language. This chapter identifies a range of perspectives and outlines the differences between them. The most well-known of these, the sub-cultural or difference approach, argues that there is an identifiable women's style of speaking. Other theoretical positions, the dominance approach and, more recently, the postmodernist approach, challenge its proponents, pointing to similarities between its claims and those of non-feminist or pre-feminist views. These key positions are outlined in order to help readers through the summary of research findings in Chapter 6.

Chapter 6 examines the evidence and counter-evidence for the claim that language use is determined by **sex** or gender. Research findings are schematically summarized under three headings, namely phonology and grammar; lexis and pragmatic particles; and discourse. Two exercises are included for readers to test for themselves whether women and men differ with regard to their vocabulary. The discussion on research findings focuses on methodology and research design. Does our understanding of gender affect our research design? Can research design bias our results? How do we interpret results? How can we control for factors other than gender which may affect our results when we design an experiment?

Chapter 7 provides a further and more detailed critique of sex-difference research, this time focusing not on academic work but on popular best-sellers in the book market. It will show the links between these self-help books aimed at heterosexual women in failing marriages and the assertiveness-training movement for women in industry and business, and challenge the underlying idea that changing communication style can fundamentally alter the material forces which underpin inequality in marriage and at work.

Chapter 8 summarizes the main conclusions of the book and includes a short examination of one form of feminist resistance: humour. It shows how humour pinpoints social attitudes to women, men and the relationships between them, and how it stereotypes the women and men who are the targets of jokes. It ends with suggestions as to the direction of further research, specifically by arguing for a focus on power and violence. Like all the preceding chapters, it includes suggestions for further reading. A bibliography of all the references cited has been added. Readers are advised to follow up on particular interests by referring to these original sources. A glossary of technical or specialized terms is appended at the end of the book.

Summary

- language is central to all human interaction and no one interested in social change can ignore how it works

- feminists' views on language and its contribution to the oppression of women differ according to their conceptions of gender and its relation to other social categories

- there are three feminist positions identified in the literature of linguistics: a dominance position, a difference position and a postmodernist position, roughly mapping on to a range of feminist theories

- the category of gender itself, central to many feminist positions, is now challenged by postmodernist theorists

- the postmodernist challenge to gender affects interpretation of data in feminist sociolinguistics

Further reading

Cameron, Deborah 1985 *Feminism and linguistic theory*, Macmillan, London, Chapter 7, pp. 114–133.

Bing, Janet M. and Bergvall, Victoria L. 1996 'The question of questions: beyond binary thinking', in Bergvall, V.L., Bing, J.M. and Freed, A.F. (eds) *Rethinking language and gender research: theory and practice*, Addison Wesley Longman, New York, pp. 1–30.

Delphy, Christine 1984 *Close to home: A materialist analysis of women's oppression*, Hutchinson, London. See especially chapter on Annie Leclerc's 'Parole de Femme' entitled 'Proto-feminism and anti-feminism'.

PART ONE

Chapter 2

Analyzing language from a feminist perspective

Chapter outline

This chapter introduces key terms and concepts used throughout Part I. It aims to

- raise awareness about language
- outline in brief the most important theories and models in linguistic analysis
- provide an introduction to the study of gender in language, comparing English with other languages
- show how language reflects social hierarchies and political structures
- introduce the study of metaphor and its relation to conceptualization

This book is aimed at a wide audience of readers who are not necessarily familiar with linguistics or with feminist theory. This chapter will introduce the key items, theories and models of language needed to understand the concerns feminists have in their search to investigate the connection between language and the social system which favours males. The discipline of linguistics is a quickly expanding one, and it is certainly beyond the scope of this introductory text to give an adequate account of the entire field. Many good introductions exist (e.g. Aitchison 1992). This chapter intends to select only those areas of import to a feminist approach. Relatively advanced texts and readers from a feminist perspective also exist (e.g. Cameron 1985, Cameron 1990).

Language: theories and models

Language has been studied for thousands of years but the way it is now studied, as a scientific discipline, can be dated to the posthumous publication of Swiss linguist Ferdinand de Saussure's lecture course by his students in 1916. His *Cours de Linguistique Générale* was instrumental in establishing linguistics as a discipline in its own right, with its own focus, language. Saussure's ideas were largely about language as an abstraction: he divided it into two components, *langue* (language as a system of signs) and *parole* (speech or language in use), and it was the sign system to which he devoted his intellectual energies. He called this study semiology.

Saussure viewed the sign as a combination of a signifier (sound and spelling of a word) and a signified (concept). One of his most important observations was that the relationship between the two is arbitrary, that is, while in English a barking, tail-wagging mammal is called a *dog*, in French it is *chien*, and in German *Hund*. If all English speakers decided as of tomorrow to call it a *proz*, it would not matter. A child learning the language would learn to label all tail-wagging, barking animals a *proz* and later come to learn that *proz* is *chien* in French, *cu* in Welsh and *mádra* in Irish. All of our words are arbitrary in this way, except perhaps onomatopoeic words like *woof-woof, miaow, plop* and *splash*, which represent the English language speech community's attempt to use the voice to copy non-human sound. Even **onomatopoeia** is revealed as culture specific: Japanese rain doesn't go 'pitter-patter' at all.

So the signifier is arbitrary, and a rose by another name would smell as sweet. Further, the signified (concepts, ideas) is also arbitrary to a certain extent. We do not name everything in the world around us. What we *do* name helps us to notice and talk about it. In *Drawing on the right side of the brain* (1979), artist and art teacher Betty Edwards shows how switching off our language centre (left brain), enables us to draw far more accurately. She argues that in drawing, say, a face, we draw stereotypical 'eyes' 'nose' 'lips' and fail to see correctly. She suggests we try instead to draw the space between outer nostril, say, and edge of mouth, a part of the face without a name, or other negative spaces. Words interfere in seeing the whole; words make us focus on parts. Taken to extremes, this insight that we arbitrarily name some but not all of the undifferentiated mass of sense impressions we receive, leads to linguistic relativity or **determinism**. This is the argument that different languages 'carve up' the world in different ways, and that the language we speak will influence – or even determine – how we view and conceive of reality. This has interested some feminists a great deal: if language is sexist and influences us to think in sexist ways, then language reform can help change sexist social arrangements. This is discussed in Chapter 3.

We have seen that signs are arbitrary, that is the sound or written form of a word bears no relation to the thing it stands for or signifies. What does matter is that they should all be different from each other. We cannot call a cat, a dog, a table and a fridge a *ploz*, or else we would be constantly confused. Sounds can combine in many different ways. Compare *dog, dig, dug*, or *cat, mat, sat.* Our language works as a signalling system because signs can combine in sequences to make words, sentences, texts and can differ from each other to produce meaning.

Feminists, especially French feminists, have developed Saussure's insights into language as a system of signs, as has French psychoanalyst Jacques Lacan who argues that the unconscious is structured like a language, i.e. as a sign system. The consequences of this are enormous in the role language plays in the making of each individual subject. This is discussed later in brief. For a more detailed presentation see Cameron (1985), Marks and De Courtivron (1981), Moi (1985).

The dominant linguistic paradigm or framework since the late 1950s is that associated with American linguist, Chomsky. Like Saussure, Chomsky divided up language into two, corresponding roughly to *langue* and *parole*. Chomsky called these *competence* and *performance.* Like Saussure, Chomsky has been mainly interested in an abstraction: the language rules of an ideal speaker–hearer speaking standard English. The main concern of Chomskyan linguistics has been to write a complete set of rules for making correct sentences in a language. Language users are creative; we constantly make up sentences which have never been heard or said before, yet we are understood. Our performance (actual speech) is understood because our hearers share with us the knowledge about how to form acceptable sentences in our particular language (competence). The focus in Chomskyan linguistics has been on syntax, word order in sentences and on rules to explain how we can generate new sentences from our rules, by making transformations in the structure of sentences.

Feminists have been little concerned to engage in this type of linguistics. As it is concerned with language as an abstraction and tends to view actual production (performance) as typically flawed,

and since it has little to say about how language produces meaning, interacts with our knowledge of the world or with social systems, it is not very useful for a person concerned with how language
serves women, describes women or how women use language.
Hence, feminists have tended to be more interested in the spoken
form than the written, and in language produced in real life rather
than the imagined sentences derived by native-speaker intuition.

Real-life communication differs quite markedly from that
described by models using the notion of a perfectly shared code
between ideal speaker–hearers. In reality, misunderstandings occur
due to a wide variety of factors: we sometimes fail to hear what our
interlocutor is saying; we choose the wrong words for what we
(thought we) wanted to say; our attention may lapse; we forget
what we said earlier or what our interlocutor said, and so on. An
approach which focuses on the sentence as the unit of analysis
cannot deal adequately with naturally occurring conversation. We
do not, or rarely do we, speak in sentences. A focus on language in
use needs other frameworks of analysis than that of sentence types.

Discourse analysis, conversation analysis, **sociolinguistics**, **critical
linguistics** and social semiotic approaches to language are more
useful frameworks for those interested in the interaction between
language and social structure. The analysis of conversation and
sociolinguistics in general are discussed in Part II. Here, I will
focus on introducing the terms and ideas which feminists have
been able to use and develop in working on the analysis of texts.
In order to begin to see what can be done by feminists who work
on analyzing language, we need a model of what language is. The
straightforward flow of perfectly understood information from one
person to another it clearly is not. This model seems to leave something out. That something is context.

Language and social context

> Our model for communication is the conversation among a group
> of friends helping one another to move an awkward piece of
> furniture.
>
> (Mühlhäusler and Harré 1990: 12)

Halliday and Hasan make the same point in a more general way:

To study language then, is to concentrate upon exploring how it is systematically patterned towards important social ends.

(1989: vii)

In other words, language does not exist in a (social) vacuum. Before any utterance is made or sentence written, there is a set of circumstances – a context – operating. This context precedes the text, the language produced, and it inflects the language produced. This view of language was developed by Firth (1935) and Hymes (1972) who specified what was meant by context. The form and content of a message (utterance, text of any kind) depend upon setting, participants (speakers, writers, hearers, readers), the aim or intention and effect of the interaction, the medium (speech, radio, print), the genre (dinner conversation, service encounter, news broadcast, novel) and community norms of interaction. One obvious way in which such an analysis can appeal to feminists is the focus on participants. Who says what to whom in what circumstances and for what purpose? Feminists interested in breaking down stereotypes of 'women's speech' have, for example, shown how status rather than sex can determine speaking patterns, and that linguistic features such as pragmatic particles, viewed as signals of deference or hesitation, may in fact have other functions (see Chapters 5 and 6). Context is everything.

The British school of linguistics, or Hallidayan linguistics, is centrally concerned with context of situation. It aims to develop and elaborate a text linguistics which focuses on the 'systematic relationship between the social environment on the one hand, and the functional organization of language on the other' (Halliday and Hasan 1989: 11). Text is understood as language with a function, not just words but meanings. Meanings involve interpretation, which depends upon knowledge of the world. This makes hearing, reading and other forms of exchange a process rather than a thing. It also breaks with the old literary tradition of seeking meaning in authorial intention. Feminist discourse analysts and stylisticians, such as Mills (1995), have focused on analyzing language at the level of word, sentence and text to examine how meaning is produced. Meaning does not reside unproblematically in words and sentences; rather we produce meaning in the act of reading or hearing, and we do so in cognizance of context. Such a view of language and communication is a far cry from the rather mechanistic one which views it as a kind of telementation, or passage of one (perfectly formed) thought from one mind to another.

Whereas for Chomsky, transformation of basic sentences into other forms was innocent, for Kress and Hodge (1979: 9) transformations serve to distort. Some examples of particular interest to feminists are the use of the passive voice rather than the active voice, nominalization, transitivity and the manipulation of given and new information in the structure of sentences (Mills 1995: 12). Work on structures such as these attempts to show how language can be used to suggest preferred or dominant meanings, to manipulate consensus, to reinforce particular beliefs about social arrangements such as beliefs about women and men, and to distort understanding by failing to focus on processes in favour of a focus on things or essences. Let us look at some examples.

Clark (1992) is a study of the reporting of crimes of sexual violence upon women in *The Sun*, a British tabloid newspaper, in which the author examines language used in the articles relating to rape and other sexual assaults to determine who is blamed for these crimes. She uses naming analysis (see Chapter 4) to see how victims are categorized and labelled and also how attackers are viewed, noting the latter are sometimes defined by using **metaphors** suggesting sub-human status.

Clark develops Halliday's (1985) model of transitivity (Halliday and Hasan 1989) to analyze the attribution of responsibility. Transitivity relates to the components of clauses (the people involved, the circumstances, and the acts or processes described). The best way to see how such analysis works is perhaps to focus on a headline actually present in her corpus and compare it with one she invented:

GIRL 7 MURDERED WHILE MUM DRANK AT THE PUB
(*The Sun* 20/12/86, p. 7 in Clark 1992: 213)

FIEND STRANGLES ONLY CHILD, 7 [headline]
Divorced Mum grieves alone [sub-heading] (ibid: 214)

Whereas Clark's invented headline uses an active sentence, identifying the murderer, and thus making him responsible (linguistically), *The Sun* report uses passivization and agent deletion. The 'doer' or agent has been removed from the headline by using the passive form of the verb 'to murder'. Moreover, by adding 'while Mum drank at the pub', blame is shifted to the absent mother. Nothing is said about the murderer, nor, for that matter, about the absent father.

Passivization and **agent** deletion are commonly used in scientific texts. Reports of psychology experiments are, for example,

replete with examples of passive forms or nominalized forms, as
are medical texts. Feminists have argued that such forms have
the effect of allowing the agent to disappear from the surface
of the text, making them 'unrecoverable'. Compare the following
sentences:

The rat was then injected with morphine.
(Passive)

Then I injected the rat with morphine.
(Active)

The next step was the administration of morphine by injection.
(Nominalization)

With the active form, the process is transparent: an agent, 'I' injects
a creature, the rat, with a substance. With the passive form, the
agent has been deleted. With **nominalization**, the process, the action,
has been made into a thing in a timeless frame. In Chapter 4, this
idea is explored further in a short exercise on the words 'prostitution' and 'surrogate motherhood'. A strong critique of the passive
voice is made by Daly:

> The passive voice calls us from all sides. It is embedded in the
> voices of the secret agents, manipulators, possessors, who use
> passive forms not only to disguise *who* are the agents of androcracy,
> but also to pacify/passivize its victims/patients.

> (1978: 324)

When the agent is unrecoverable from the surface of a passive
sentence, there may be an appeal to universal consensus, or else
the result may be our inability as readers/hearers to pinpoint the
person/s responsible for an action. Students of science are taught
not to use 'I', to narrate or to use metaphor in writing reports, all
in the aim of appearing objective. Writers easily manipulate consensus by prefacing their opinions with such phrases as 'It is well
known that . . .' or 'It has long been established that . . .'. Often,
these mean 'I think'.

Passivization can also apply to adjectives. In my work on the language used by doctors in reproductive technology (Gibbon 1996),
I found numerous examples of such adjectives. Doctors routinely
select patients to avail of these technologies on the basis of social,
as well as medical, criteria. Depending on the country involved
'suitability' will depend upon marital status and sexual orientation, age, income, medical history and attitude. Doctors' guidelines
refer to couples deemed *suitable* (suitable to whom?), state that

it is *desirable* for the woman to give up work, and *undesirable* for patients to ask too many questions. Adjectives like these can even be made into nouns: a recent residents' committee leaflet warned of the imminent arrival in my neighbourhood of *undesirables.*

Thus, when we use language, we make choices and choices are not always innocent, but determined by belief systems which underlie them. We can be more or less aware of them, such as when we correct ourselves in speaking, perhaps to choose a more politically correct expression (see Chapter 4). We are more often aware of them in listening to others speak, as when we challenge a person's formulation. A woman aware of the negative associations the word *abortion* has for many, may prefer to use *termination* as a euphemism in certain company. Anti-abortionists, on the other hand, consider *abortion* a euphemism for *murder* of the *pre-born,* a term they invented to raise the status of the foetus. It is to words and word meaning we now turn.

Words, word meaning and social context

Within linguistics, words and meaning are discussed differently according to the sub-branch of the discipline involved. Etymology looks at the history of words and at word change. **Lexicography** – the compiling of dictionaries and glossaries – is mainly interested in cataloguing and defining the words in a language at a given moment. Phonology focuses on the sounds and pronunciation of words, and semantics on word meaning.

In order to have any degree of shared understanding when we communicate, we have to agree on what a word means. This agreement is never total, as we saw in relation to the word *abortion.* When a word's meaning is in dispute, we often tend to suggest looking it up in a dictionary. Feminists angered by women's exclusion from so-called **generic masculine** terms like *Man, Mankind,* have been advised to look them up in a dictionary. If we do, we find that such words 'really do' include women. Word meaning, like the meaning of a sentence or text, cannot be found in dictionaries. Language changes constantly and dictionaries take a long time to be written: when published, they are invariably out of date. Although computer technology has now made it possible to compile dictionaries using real examples from speech and print, such corpus dictionaries are still the exception. Most dictionaries give definitions and examples invented by compilers (native speaker intuition) or use contextual fragments from revered authors (who may well be long deceased). Words change meaning over time for many reasons. If enough people begin to use a word to mean something other than its current dictionary meaning, then that word 'means' what those users intend. 'Prevaricate' and 'aggravate' are two words undergoing change.

A more spectacular change is that occurring among American teenagers and under thirties adults with regard to the word *like*. Linguists divide words into lexical or content words and grammatical or functional words. The new usage of *like* as a quotative gives us an example of a lexical word being grammaticalized. In the sentence

> 'And she said to me "no way" and I'm like "hello-o?!!" '

like functions in a way similar to *I said*, hence its term, a quotative. So does *like* now mean *I said, she/he said*, etc. as well as meaning *similar to* and *to appreciate*? Well, yes it does, if you are under thirty, American or an avid fan of 'Friends' and other American cultural imports.

When linguists use the word 'mean' they separate out two kinds of meaning, denotation and connotation. If we hear a speaker utter the sentence 'And I'm like, "hello-o?!!" ' we can analyze the meaning of *like* in these two ways. If we share the code, we can say *like* here denotes *I said*. Upon hearing it, we also make assumptions about the person speaking: *like* here connotes young, possibly American speaker. If I use the word *cleck*, unless you are Welsh, it will denote nothing to you. It is a regional term meaning to tell tales on someone. Nonetheless, it may connote Welshness or regional origin. Similarly, even if *human chorionic gonadotrophin* denotes nothing to you, it will connote learnedness, science or possibly medicine.

Feminists have been acutely aware of connotation, arguing that many terms denoting women come, over time, to take on negative connotations, especially sexual. What is involved in such change is an overlayering of hostile social attitudes towards women on to the words or expressions. This 'semantic derogation' of women (Schultz [1975] 1990) involves the degeneration of positive or neutral terms into terms of abuse or ridicule. These dysphemistic (opposite of euphemistic) terms are often metaphorical in nature. Slang and abusive words for women refer to us as animals, vessels, meat, body parts and items of clothing (bitch, bag, piece of ass,

grade A meat, skirt). Feminists who link feminist analysis to ecological thought point out parallels between the derogation of
women and the appropriation of nature (Shiva 1988, Griffin 1978).
Linguistically this occurs through metaphor, the human ability
to see connections, similarity and analogy between apparently
unrelated phenomena.

Language, gender and metaphor

As we have seen, words are used to represent things. Apart
from representation, language also serves to categorize. Linguistic
relativity (see Chapter 3) argues that different cultures divide up
reality in different ways and that this is reflected in language.
Each child, as she/he learns to speak, acquires the 'way of seeing'
of the community through language.

Women have been at the forefront of research on categorization. It has been claimed that women have been interested in typ-
icality and prototype research because they inhabit the margins
of the category 'Man' (Chapter 3). This research argues that one of
our cognitive and linguistic habits is to put things into categories.
Work on colour terms exploits the notion that some reds are more
red than others, for example (Berlin and Kay 1969). Pillarbox red
(to use an ethnocentric example – Irish pillar boxes being green!)
is considered by most people to be the basic red, a more representative red than, say, crimson or cherry. It is said to be the prototype or 'best example' (Rosch 1977). Turquoise is a poor example of
blue because it is on the fuzzy boundary between blue and green.

Feminists have used prototypicality to show how men and men's
experience have been coded linguistically to be central, leading
to the exclusion, invisibility or marginality of women. Language
reflects a male-as-norm or MAN bias. So pervasive is this norm in
language and in thought that language reform may be doomed to
failure. If when we see neutral terms like *people, human being, adult,
person, citizen, voter, resident* we still conjure up a male, then attacks
on words with *man* in them seem pointless.

Feminists have shown that the male-as-norm principle is at
work among translators moving between languages without gender,
such as Finnish, and languages with grammatical or conventional
gender, such as German or with so-called 'natural' gender, such
as English (Braun 1995). The same is true in translating between

French and English. In Gibbon (1995), I showed how student translators made assumptions about the gender of ambiguous referents such as *friend, neighbour* and *traveller* in translating into French. The assumption most commonly made was that the person referred to was male. The male-as-norm principle was so strong as to over-ride information from the context suggesting a female referent. Thus, in my data from over a hundred students, many referred to a pregnant teacher and *his colleague* in translating from French! (French possessives agree with the thing possessed, not the possessor, thus *son collègue* can mean her or his colleague). Braun similarly found *he* appearing in stereotypically feminine activities, like washing floors and crying (1997: 15). Thus, it appears that most languages, however they encode females and males, display male bias, although Hardman's (1996) comparison of English and Jaqi suggests that it is possible to have a language (and a culture) which does not postulate sexism as a given to be expressed. Thus, while in English, names and terms for women are derived from men's (Patrick–Patricia, host–hostess) no such derivation exists in Jaqi, an Andean language. There is no number, ranking or comparison in the language.

Hardman also takes issue with what she sees as masculine metaphors underlying the conceptual systems of Western cultures and languages: metaphors of war, conquest and violence in science, metaphors of male sexuality in academia. In fact, sexual metaphor is central even to the categorization of words: the 'genitals of speech' (Herder [1772] cited in Baron 1986: 91). Baron argues that the application of a sexual metaphor to grammar (the marking of nouns, adjectives, articles, pronouns as masculine, feminine or neuter) has coloured the way commentators have looked at linguistic representations of reality (ibid: 90). According to Baron, the history of gender in language has never been satisfactorily explained, although commentators have been working on just such an explanation at least since the sixth century. The term *gender* from Latin *genus* meaning sort, kind, type or race, has come to mean masculine, feminine and neuter when applied to the noun classes of European languages.

English is said to be a natural gender language. This means that the pronouns *he, she* and *it* refer to males, females and inanimates respectively. These three pronouns, along with their derived and related forms *her, hers, him, his, its,* are all that remain in English to mark gender, apart from a few **morphemes** like *-ess* and *-ette*, which feminists have rightly attacked as suffixes connoting deviation, amateurism and triviality. Theoretically, then, *she* is applied to animate females including women and girls; *he* to animate males, including men and boys; and *it* is applied to all inanimates and animates whose sex is unknown. In practice, this is not always the case, and many inanimates are ascribed a sex: cars, ships, planes and machines are often *she,* as are countries, cities, natural geographic features and symbolic representations of nations (Romaine 1997, Baron 1986). Feminists have taken issue with this practice, considered to be largely the prerogative of men. I have yet to hear a woman call her car *she* or refer to a country as *she.* I have, however, heard many women, men and children refer to most animals as *he,* including insects whose sex doesn't seem all that obvious. This is no doubt an example of the male-as-norm principle. Recently, I was amused to hear a pharmacist's sales-assistant refer to a Band-Aid sticking plaster as 'this little guy'. Clearly, metaphor is involved in ascribing sex to inanimates in this way. Such personalization is used to connote human characteristics, and adjectives normally collocated with human subjects may also be ascribed to things. Thus, a fabric may be *sweet* and *dainty* and a picture totally *darling* in the speech of certain individuals. In fact, such usage is part of the stereotype of women's speech (Chapter 6).

Whereas English, a predominantly natural gender language, marks gender only in some suffixes, pronouns and possessive adjectives, most other European languages are based on conventional or grammatical gender. French, for example, divides up all beings and all things, including abstract concepts like time, space, freedom and intelligence, into feminine or masculine categories. For animates, gender generally agrees with sex. Thus a woman and a girl are *une femme, une fille* and a man and boy *un homme, un garçon.* The corresponding definite articles are *la* and *le* or *l'* before a vowel. The plurals *des* (some) and *les* (the) are unmarked for gender. The pronoun system is similar to that of English, though the third person plural, corresponding to gender neutral *they* in English is marked for gender: *elles* and *ils* for female and male subjects respectively. Unlike English, French possessive adjectives are not marked according to the possessor (*her/his*). The equivalent terms *son/sa/ses* change according to the following noun's gender. Thus before *mère* (mother) we must use *sa* (*sa mère*: her mother or his mother), before *père* (father) we use *son* (*son père*: her father or his father) and so on. Other Romance languages are similar.

German, on the other hand, retains the three-way system English displays in its residual form. All German nouns are divided into feminine (*die*), masculine (*der*) or neuter (*das*). Like French, adjectives also agree with nouns. Thus, gender marking is highly redundant in grammatical gender languages, as can be seen from a simple example. Let us compare some English phrases with their equivalent French translations:

> The small girl
> La (f) petite (f) fille (f)
>
> The small boy
> Le (m) petit (m) garçon (m)
>
> A small child
> Un (m) petit (m) enfant (m)

Linguists use the term 'marked' to refer to the feminine adjectives used in these French examples. The 'e' at the end of *petite* marks feminine gender. *Petit*, the masculine form, is considered unmarked, or basic. Of course, this reflects male-as-norm ideas, similar to those at work in the prescriptivists' rule that *he* encompasses *he* and *she* or that *mankind* is generic in meaning. Looking again at our three phrases we note something similar in French: the word for child is masculine and although *une enfant* does exist, it can only refer to a girl. *Un enfant*, however, is a generic masculine term, showing that the masculine, in French, is a default gender. Although third person plural subject pronouns *elles* and *ils* refer to females and males, for a mixed group the masculine is used. The presence of one male two-year-old is enough to turn a group of fifty women into *ils*. In languages where one female in a group of ten men requires the use of a female plural pronoun, it is said one woman is enough to 'contaminate' the group. Feminist language reformers face different kinds of problems depending on the way their language marks gender. For grammatical gender languages like French and German, the move is towards increased feminization, while English-speaking feminists work towards neutralization (see Chapter 4).

A study of European languages alone is inadequate to understand the importance of **metaphor** as an underlying organizing principle for human conceptualization. In European languages gender does seem to map on to sex, at least for animates. Other languages categorize nouns into groups too, and although linguists use the term *gender* (remember it meant *type* originally) to describe the noun classifications of languages, biological sex and its extension to things is not the only principle found. (For a thorough discussion of noun classifications in the world's languages, see Corbett 1991). Some systems depend on sound combined with gender (Italian, Irish). Others have what appears far more exotic motivation.

One of the most commonly cited languages in the linguistics and anthropology literature is Dyirbal, a language spoken by native Australians (Dixon 1972, Lakoff 1987). Already at the time Dixon described the language, its noun classification and its underlying conceptual system, Dyirbal culture was under threat, and with it the language, including its noun classes. Dixon identified a four-way split, making immediate nonsense of any idea of sex-gender as a pure underlying principle. For Dyirbal speakers, all nouns were divided into one of four types. This may appear simple compared with the twenty or so types or genders in some African languages. However, in order to understand the noun class system, it is essential to understand the culture and mythology behind it. Men and most animals including fish are in the *bayi* class. Europeans call this Class I. Say no more. Class II, *balan*, is for women, birds, the moon and a creature with a nasty bite, as well as fire and all things hot. Class III groups edible foods and Class IV is a residue or 'rag-bag' group for words which do not fit into any of the other three by analogy. Fishing rods relate to fish and go into Class I. The garfish, dangerous to humans, goes in with women, fire and other dangerous things. Younger speakers no longer share the cultural beliefs and knowledge of their ancestors and elders and the system is being reduced to one remarkably like the European masculine, feminine, neuter system.

Romaine (1997) rephrasing Penelope (1990) points out that although Dyirbal seems strange to English speakers, similar metaphors are at work in English. Hurricanes, until recently, were systematically given female names; nature is personified as female in Mother Nature and viewed as an irrational and potentially destructive force to be controlled and subdued by man/men. Certainly such metaphors were rife in Enlightenment science with Bacon promising to put nature 'on the rack', wrest from her all her secrets and mine her entrails for them. Contemporary embryologists and doctors in reproductive technology share with Bacon some gruesome metaphors for women and women's bodies, writing as they do of 'mining' women of their eggs or 'harvesting', 'collecting' and 'retrieving' them, and the technologies themselves are as invasive as the vocabulary suggests.

In a paper on metaphor and technology, Wilson (1992) argues that:

> Our conceptual systems are fundamentally metaphorical in nature and play a role in defining everyday reality. Language, in particular metaphor, helps form social reality.
>
> (1992: 883)

The worlds of science and technology have been described as representing a 'chilly climate' for women. According to Wilson, science and technology's basic metaphors contribute to this, by constituting women as other, and by drawing analogies with pursuits deemed masculine: war, conquest, exploration and religion.

Box 2.1 Feminine and masculine categories

While a great deal of feminist attention has been paid to words (denotation and connotation) and to grammar (pronouns, he/man language), relatively little has been written on metaphor. Yet it appears that English speakers do categorize things from ships and cars to sticking plasters into feminine and masculine categories. You can try this out by conducting a small experiment. Try asking friends or classmates to assign a female or male label to pairs of words to see if they see them as more female than male and vice versa. For example, try the following to see if you find agreement, or make up some of your own:

whiskey	gin
milk	coffee
brown	lemon
curry	casserole
quiche	steak sandwich
weeping willow	oak tree
daisy	lupin

Moreover, metaphorical thinking potentially has effects in the material world. Rape victims and anorexic women are encouraged to see therapists. Underlying this is a view of rape as an illness. The therapeutic model encourages us to view rape and anorexia as medical or psychological problems, rather than social and political ones. Another form of agent deletion perhaps?

Summary

- the words of a language have both a representational function and a categorizational function

- modern linguistics focuses on language as system and language in use, and feminists are particularly interested in its use in social context

- speaking and writing involve making choices about linguistic forms; these are not neutral but socially and politically motivated

- however a language encodes gender, male bias is possible in language use, suggesting language reform may be doomed

- a feminist study of metaphor reveals sexist bias in English categorization in a wide range of disciplines and professions

Further reading

Toolan, Michael (ed.) 1992 *Language, text and context: Essays in stylistics*, Routledge, London, especially Part III: 'Positioning styles: framing women in language', Chapters 8 and 9.

Cameron, Deborah 1985 *Feminism and linguistic theory*, Macmillan, London, Chapters 1 and 2.

Baron, Dennis 1986 *Grammar and gender*, Yale University Press, New Haven, Chapter 6.

Lakoff, George and Johnson, M. 1980 *Metaphors we live by*, University of Chicago Press, Chicago.

McConnell-Ginet, Sally 1979 'Prototypes, pronouns and persons', in Mathiot Madeleine (ed.) *Ethnolinguistics: Boas, Sapir and Whorf revisited*, Mouton, The Hague.

Chapter 3

Language, thought and reality: feminist perspectives

Chapter outline

This chapter looks at the theoretical underpinnings of feminist views on the relationship between culture and language.

Its aims are

- to introduce the question of the relationship between language, reality and thought
- to present feminist views on the relationships between language, thought and social reality
- to explore these issues by means of an investigation of the English pronoun *he* (epicene or prescriptive *he*) and of generic masculine noun forms
- to examine the effects of androcentric language in education and the law
- to introduce the idea of inscribing women's meanings in language

Language, thought and reality

Feminists are far from the first thinkers to grapple with the question of the relationship between language, thought and reality. Anthropologists and linguists have been debating the issues for most of this century. Two thinkers, Edward Sapir and Benjamin Whorf, are credited with the idea that we apprehend reality through language so that language influences – or even determines – how we think and how we perceive reality. This idea, which has come to be called the Sapir–Whorf hypothesis is, strictly speaking, not a hypothesis. It has been claimed that it is untestable (Herriot 1970). Nor is it Sapir and Whorf's. Vendler (1977) traces the idea back to Plato, quoting a famous passage in *Theaetetus:*

> Socrates: And do you accept my description of the process of thinking?
> Theaetetus: How do you describe it?
> Socrates: As a discourse that the mind carries on with itself about any subject it is considering. You must take this explanation as coming from an ignoramus; but I have a notion that, *when the mind is thinking, it is simply talking to itself,* asking questions and answering them. . . . So I should describe thinking as a discourse, and judgement as a statement pronounced, not aloud to someone else, but silently to oneself.
> (cited in Hamilton and Cairns 1963: 895–6, my italics)

This question reflects the position that language and thought are one: thinking is talking to oneself. Those who oppose the notion that language and cognition are so intricately connected view the mind in a more modular fashion, arguing largely that cognition is a separate function from language, that we think in 'mentalese'. Steven Pinker gives a modern version of this idea in his book *The Language Instinct,* after a passage where he pours scorn on the **Sapir–Whorf hypothesis:**

> We have all had the experience of uttering or writing a sentence, then stopping and realizing that it wasn't exactly what we meant to say. To have that feeling, there has to be a 'what we meant to say' that is different from what we said. Sometimes it is not easy to find <u>any</u> words that properly convey a thought. When we hear or read, we usually remember the gist, not the exact words, so there has to be such a thing as a gist that is not the same as a bunch of words. And if thoughts depended on words, how could a new word ever be coined? How could a child learn a word to begin with? How could translation from one language to another be possible?
> (1994: 57–8)

Just as the Sapir–Whorf idea is not new, neither are the positions of its detractors. Aristotle argued that while humans have a variety of languages, they still all think the same way:

> Spoken words are the symbols of mental experience and written words are the symbols of spoken words. Just as all men have not

the same writing, so all men have not the same speech sounds, but the *mental experiences, which they directly symbolize, are the same for all,* as also are those things of which our experience are the images.
(*De Interpretatione* 16 a, in McKeon 1968: 40, my italics)

Nowadays, the Sapir–Whorf hypothesis, or the notion of linguistic relativity, remains controversial. While in its strong form (language determines thought) it has few supporters, in its weaker form it has many. Henle (1958: 18) puts forward a weak version:

Language is one of the factors influencing perception and the general organisation of experience. This influence need not be primary or unique or compelling, but neither is it negligible.

Sapir and Whorf themselves offered strong and weak versions of the hypothesis at different times and based their assertions upon different features of language, Sapir giving largely lexical items as proof (at least initially), while Whorf focused on the grammatical features of the native American language, Hopi. He examined its tense system, or relative lack of one, and its conjunctions which suggested to him that the Hopi language was a more suitable one for philosophizing than Indo-European languages like English, German or French. Whorf's argument was, unfortunately, used in racist propaganda in the 1930s, but his own position was anything but racist. The development of the linguistic relativity thesis did have the effect of raising the status of linguistics among anthropologists and increasing funding for linguistic research.

One of the most commonly discussed areas of difference in vocabulary across cultures is that of colour. Whereas it has been shown that all humans without vision problems have the same perceptual abilities, and that we therefore all see the same range of hues, luminosity and saturation (the three properties of colour), the naming of colour in different cultures shows enormous variation. An extensive study of ninety-eight languages (Berlin and Kay 1969) showed that languages divided into twenty-two groups, according to the number of different colour terms they used. Interestingly, the addition of colour terms to a group's lexicon follows a relatively set pattern: group 1 has just two terms (white and black); group 2 has white, black and red; group 3 adds yellow and green, and so on up to group 6, representing speakers of Indo-European languages which mostly have eleven: the colours of the rainbow, white and black, pink, brown, and grey.

Clearly, western cultures need a wide range of colour terms; think of being an electrician without brown, blue, green and yellow for wiring, or of traffic lights, or of the textile dyeing industry. We would find it hard to manage with the three terms of many African cultures, just as they would find it hard to negotiate their kith and kin relationships with our impoverished kinship terms (Gourvès-Hayward 1998: 209). How would we manage with, say, the three colour terms of Gouro (an Ivory Coast language)? They use *ti*, (black) *fou*, (white) and *son* (red). It is simple to devise an exercise to see just what a perceptual and categorization leap is required to classify our world in just three colours.

Box 3.1 Colour classification

Exercise (devised by Gourvès-Hayward)

For this exercise, you need to make up a handout with colour chips, of the kind provided by paint stores, or use the one provided here at the end of this chapter. First, try naming all the colours in English. Then try classifying them into the eleven basic colours used in English: white, black, red, yellow, green, blue, brown, purple, pink, orange, grey. Check your answers with those of your classmates. Disagreements may emerge around the blue/green boundary and the red/orange/yellow boundary. Now, using the same colours, try classifying them as *ti*, *fou* or *son*. Then check your answers against the key.

What you will find is that intensity and brightness underlies the Gouro colour classification system: all dark colours and all blues and greens are *ti* (black); warm shades like reds, pinks, yellows are *son* (red) unless very pale or very dark; all very pale colours are *fou* (white).

Exercise key

Number on chip	American paint-shop label	Gouro term
1	Picked plum	ti
2	Greenway	ti
3	Fire Princess	son
4	Sun Valley	son
5	Gloucester Sage	ti
6	English Rose	ti
7	Wistaria Blue	fou
8	Sunlit Sea	ti
9	Marine Blue	ti
10	Lemon Ice	son

11	Shenanigin	ti
12	Carriage Red	ti
13	Nectarine	son
14	Parasol Pink	son
15	Hash Brown	ti
16	Calico Blue	ti
17	Jet Black	ti
18	Spectrum Red	son
19	Gray Button	ti
20	Tiger Lily	son
21	Little Boy Blue	ti
22	Spectrum Yellow	son
23	Rose Breath	son
24	Purple Ribbon	ti
25	Brown Rose	ti
26	Mosaic Blue	ti
27	Primrose	ti
28	Orange Sovereign	son

You may like to do some follow-up work to this exercise. You could see what happens if you compare results with classmates or friends. Think about how you felt doing this exercise. Discuss how your life would be affected if you had to switch to a three-term colour classification system. Were there differences in the way you named these colours in English? Did these differences correlate with age, gender or involvement in hobbies? Some linguists have argued that women use a wider range of terms than men to describe colours (see Chapter 6). You may like to do some follow-up reading. Refer to bibliography at the end of the book.

Feminist views on linguistic relativity

Linguistic relativity has been of great interest to feminist linguists. If language can be shown to influence or determine thought, then sexist language will influence speakers in the direction of sexist thought. Changing sexist language will change sexist attitudes; challenging sexist language will raise awareness about sexist assumptions. Dale Spender is a prominent feminist writer who based her book *Man-made language* upon the notion that language is not just a reflection of ideas and thoughts, is not neutral, but is a trap which limits our capacity to think in non-sexist ways:

> [I]t has been the dominant group – in this case, males – who have created the world, invented the categories, constructed sexism and its justification and developed a language map which is in their interest.
>
> (1985: 142)

Spender argues in favour of the Sapir–Whorf hypothesis, quite explicitly, writing 'it is language which determines the limits of our world, which constructs our reality' (1985: 139). She develops it, not by cross-cultural comparison which is the obvious testing ground for the hypothesis, but by a close examination of lexical and grammatical categorization in English. Her aim is to show how sexist meanings are encoded in the language, leading to the marginalization of women's experience, the invisibility of women or else their derogation. A number of other feminists have also researched this question, as have mainstream linguists, focusing, as did Sapir and Whorf, on the lexicon and upon grammar. We go on to focus on these two areas, relating lexis to categorization and perception and grammatical structure to representation of women and men in language, thought and perception.

Theorists of linguistic relativity have pointed out that different cultures 'carve up' the world in different ways. Typical examples are the terms different language communities dispose of to describe colours, as we have seen, and the terms to describe relations of kinship. For example, while English has two separate words for *blue* and *green*, Welsh has one, *glas*, as does Japanese, *aoi*. Russian, on the other hand, has two separate terms corresponding to English blue, *goluboy* and *siny*. Similarly, while in English we have one word for *sister*, Japanese distinguishes lexically between older and younger sisters. Of course, to return to Pinker, we *can* translate these Japanese terms into English by using 'younger' or 'older' to qualify which sister we mean, and we *can* specify light or dark blue to translate Russian's two terms. What is clear, however, is that Japanese has two words for *sister* because the hierarchy of age is more salient in Japanese culture than in the English-speaking world. And Pinker is only partially correct and rather glib in saying we can translate. If Russian has two separate words for 'blue' corresponding to dark and light versions, how do we translate *blue* into Russian? How do we translate *sister* into Japanese, if we do not know/care whether the sister is older or younger? French can say *sister* and *brother* (*soeur/frère*) but not *sibling*; it can say *female* or *male cousin* (*cousine/cousin*) but not just '*cousin*'. If we have so many approximate equivalences in cognate languages of the same Indo-European family, how many more difficulties we might expect to encounter in translating across language pairs which are unrelated. While representational features are generally translatable, categorization often is not.

This rapid examination of a few interesting translation problems should suffice to make us see that languages can be viewed, from a lexical point of view, in terms of what they can say, cannot say and must say; and, most importantly, what they do say. So, in talking of cousins, English can say *my female cousin* or *my male cousin* to correspond to French *ma cousine, mon cousin*, but does it? We do not actually specify, so that 'I am going to stay with my female cousin in Letterkenny for the weekend' sounds distinctly odd. French must specify the sex, English can but does not. The same is true in general of terms of occupations, which in English are largely epicene, and in Romance languages marked for gender. A detailed examination of relevant aspects the lexicon of English from a feminist perspective is provided in Chapter 4, but in this section we will examine the main issues in a more general way, focusing here on generic masculine words and associated patterns of thought, linking feminist linguistics with psychology. The discussion is centred on the *man* element of he/man language and on pronouns.

Is a woman a man? Can *he* mean *she*?

> *Un homme sur deux est une femme.*
> (French feminist slogan: One man in two is a woman).

During the 1970s and early 1980s, feminists began voluntarily to alter language to reflect and to draw attention to the masculist inflections of our vocabulary. One suggested change was the re-spelling of 'woman' and 'women' (womyn/womin/wimyn/wimmin). These re-spellings reflected the urge not to derive the female form from the male form *man*. Other feminists felt the same way about the pairs male/female, arguing against this 'marking' of the feminine form. Markedness is a linguistic term referring to the addition of a morpheme (of gender, number, diminutive, etc.) to a core term viewed as unmarked or neutral. More recently Gouëffic (1996) has argued for a far more systematic recovery of authentic forms for women (fem/fems/femhood) and a deletion of all *man*-derived roots from our vocabulary both for the species and for womanhood/femhood.

Etymologically, *woman* does not derive from *man* in the way feminists have often thought, and the word *man* has not always referred to both the species and the male of the species. The generic meaning of the word *man*, that is the term to describe the species Homo Sapiens, preceded the sex-specific meaning. Its origin is contested but a number of roots in Proto- Indo-European have been suggested, deriving *man* from the root *man* for *hand*, relating it to *manufacture*, *manipulate*. Some derive it from *men* for *mind*, *mental* or from *mon*, an early form for *human being*. Most cautious etymologists trace it only back as far as its old Germanic forms. In modern German there are two words: *Mensch* (human being) and *Mann* (man, husband) while in English we have one, ambiguously referring to the adult male or to the species. However, this was not always the case. In its earlier forms, *man* referred to the species and two separate markers *wif* and *waep* were added to specify female and male. Thus *wifmann* and *waepmann*, apparently meaning *weaver person* and *weapon-carrying person*, were how women and men were named in old English. '*Wermann*' (for males) is also attested, the prefix '*wer*' (Latin *vir*) remaining in the word *werewolf* (a man-wolf).

Interesting though such etymological studies are, they tell us little about the language in use today or how people feel about it. Feminists and many other women are offended by our marginalization in the term for our species, *Man*, and this is reinforced by the pronoun *he* to refer to us. On the other hand, feminists working on etymology have been able to draw attention to the fanciful and less than disinterested musings of many male etymologists who have used prejudice rather than evidence to establish derivation of words relating to women and marriage (Baron 1986, Penelope 1990, Wolfe and Stanley 1980, Gouëffic 1996). Moreover, they have been able to provide a radical reinterpretation of Indo-European culture by a linguistic analysis of terms for kinship and account for many of the 'anomalies' of IE vocabulary, as identified by etymologists who paint the ancestral culture as patriarchal. (Wolfe and Stanley 1980: 236–7).

To return to our focus on *man* and the relationship between lexis and perception or thought, we will now examine *man* and other so-called generic-masculine words in context. Emphasis will be placed here not on dictionary meanings (denotation) but on mental imagery or the thoughts which spring up in our minds upon reading or hearing such words, and when we ourselves speak or write them. Given the scope of this introductory text, only a brief summary of research can be given. As a preliminary exercise, try writing down all the words you can think of to refer to people and ask yourself whether they can be used to refer to women, individually or as a group; to men, individually or as a group; to children; to mixed groups of adults; to mixed groups of adults and children.

The range of words is actually much greater than our species word *Man* might suggest. *Humankind, humanity, humans, the human race, people, individuals, citizens, Homo Sapiens, guys, y'all, us* and *we* are some of the terms we might come up with. Some of these (*man, guys*) are more likely than others to conjure up male imagery. Many terms which are at root masculine are intended nonetheless to include women: the clergy's use of *brethren* traditionally referred to the entire congregation (most often female-dominated); to *man* a stand at a school bazaar is often the privilege of mothers; and the words *fraternize* (from Latin, *frater*, a brother) and *patronize* (from *pater*, father) are used of women as well as men. In the nineteenth century, but also in 1997, women graduating from university have objected to being awarded Bachelor's and Master's degrees, and, as we see in Chapter 4, the professions have had to be renamed to remove masculine bias in agentives.

Box 3.2 Generic masculine words: the problems

The central feminist argument against generic masculine words is that they do not work. A generic term is a category term or hypernym. It is meant to refer to all members of a class. *Generic* and *gender* derive from Latin *genus* meaning a kind or a type. Thus, *furniture* is a generic term for the hyponyms *tables, chairs, beds* and *desks; animals* is a generic term for *fish, mammals* and *reptiles,* and *car* is a generic term for *Jaguars, Fords, Toyotas* and *Volvos.* To assess how poor *man* is a generic for human species, let us see how well it compares with the other generics mentioned:

Furniture: chair, bed, table, desk

> A chair is a piece of furniture.
> I'd like some new furniture, especially a desk.
> I'd like a new bed. Let's go furniture shopping.

Animals: fish, mammals, birds

> Humans are often carnivores; they eat all kinds of animals,
>   including fish and birds.
> Of all the animals, I like cute little mammals best.

> ### Cars: Jaguar, Ford, Toyota, Volvo
>
> > I have a Ford but if I could afford it, I'd buy a more
> > expensive car like a Jaguar.
> > Japanese cars like Toyotas are very popular second-hand cars
> > to buy in Ireland and Britain.
>
> All these generics work well, since each one can stand for any
> one of the sub-group or 'hyponyms'.
>
> ### Man: woman, man, girl, boy
>
> > ?A man is a man.
> > ?Girls and boys are man/men.
> > ?Half of all men are women.
>
> And what about these feminist inventions?:
>
> > ?Every man experiences his menstruation differently.
> > ?Man, being a mammal, breastfeeds his young.
> > ?Man, when pregnant, experiences food cravings.
> > ?Man, unlike lower mammals, has trouble giving birth.
>
> Clearly, the problem which arises in terms of our mental imagery
> is that the one word, *man*, has a specific meaning which is
> activated in our memory before, simultaneously, or just after the
> generic meaning arises, causing the 'generic' to call up male
> imagery, in other words, to fail as a generic.

Silveira reviews studies in psycholinguistic research and asserts 'the
generic *man* and *he* will make words about males easier to perceive
and produce' (1980: 173). She notes a resulting slippage between
the androcentric and generic meanings of the word *man* in much
writing, quoting Fromm (1972: 80) making precisely the kind of
association between *man* and 'male' which lies behind feminists'
dissatisfaction with the term as label for the species:

> Man can do several things that the animal cannot do . . . his vital
> interests are not only life, food, access to females, etc.

This slippage between meanings of *man* contributes to the invisibility of woman, to the framing of human experience in terms of
males' experience and the concomitant neglect of women's: It also
leads to a 'people-equals-men-unless-otherwise-specified' tendency
in language and thought. The following extract from Taylor (1974:
11–12) quoted by Gershuny in Nilsen *et al.* (1977: 53) shows meaning slippage, as well as the invisibility of women, except as womb:

Mankind has, ever since he began to think, worshipped that
which he cannot understand. As millennia have passed he has
understood an ever-increasing amount about the world around
him. He has even hoped, in his most optimistic moments, to
comprehend it all. Yet man is now in the position of facing the
ultimate unknowable which can never be penetrated as long as
he remains in his present physical form . . . The constantly
augmenting knowledge of the world has only been achieved by
centuries of dedicated work by men of science . . . it is as if man
departs from his mother's womb to enter straight into another
one created by the scientists . . . Even before birth new drugs
are used to help the foetus survive. Once born and for the
whole of his life medical discoveries allow him to drug himself,
have bad parts cut out of his body, or good ones transplanted
into it . . .
  When he has grown safely to adulthood he can wake up
in the morning in his heated or air-conditioned house, use
the latest techniques to prepare food for himself, drive off
in his heated or air-conditioned car, and spend the day in
a glass and plastic office . . . or even exceptionally be one
of the select few who have voyaged to the moon. And to cap
it all he may, if he really so desires, stay at home and change
into a she!

Numerous empirical studies have been undertaken, mostly by
social psychologists, to test the hypothesis that *man* does not function generically but causes male bias in thought. Study after study
has shown that when faced with sentences containing generic
masculine forms and/or generic *he*, subjects conjure up predominantly male images. One interesting example is Martyna's (1980)
account of a range of experiments designed to elicit interpretation of generic masculine and epicene agentives by matching
images to words, and by sentence completion exercises to test for
pronoun usage associated with such words. Martyna faults the
generic masculine on three counts: its inequity, its ambiguity and
its exclusiveness (1980: 69–70). It is this last feature which is of
most concern. If generic terms in their use or understanding actually exclude women, then they are not generic. Martyna noted
male bias, as expected, but interestingly, she also observed that
women and men in her study did not use or understand generics
in the same way. When *he* was chosen for neutral or epicene antecedents, male informants did so 'probably because I'm male' while
women did so because they argued it was correct or that they had
learned to. She concludes:

> Males may be generating a sex-specific use of *he*, one based on
> male imagery, while females are generating a truly generic *he*, one
> based on grammatical standards of correctness.
>
> (1980: 72)

Nilsen (Nilsen *et al.* 1977) had already intuited this in her discussion of sexism in children's books and class-room materials.
Using Labov's notion of Type 1 rules (automatic) and Type II rules
(learned formally) (Labov 1969: 29), Nilsen argues that girls and
boys have different experiences in relation to rules for marking
gender in lexis and grammar. A boy will, throughout infancy and
childhood, become accustomed to hearing *he, his, him* used to apply
to him while a girl hears *she, her, hers.* This affects their learning
of, and understanding, of generic *he,* taught as a Type II rule. Nilsen
conducted a range of studies with children at different stages of
their formal education to investigate their use of pronouns with
neutral antecedents like *child* and found girls tended to extrapo-
late from their own sex and use *she* while boys did the same, using
he. Nilsen notes that in adult life, *he* is used far more than *she* and
that girls have to switch their understanding of *he* to include themselves in it. Boys, on the other hand, are automatically included in
he used generically. In fact, they may well not learn to include *she*
in their pseudo-generic *he*:

> Although most men are perfectly content with the system of
> grammatical gender as it now stands, numerous studies and
> examples from usage show that they have not really learned to
> mentally include women when they use generic terms. Part of
> the evidence in support of this contention is the present state of
> confusion, with writers wavering back and forth between generic
> and literal interpretations, even within the same paragraph.
>
> (Nilsen *et al.* 1977: 178)

Given that generic *he* and *man* do not actually work in practice,
and that editors fail to correct writers' usage when it involves slid-
ing from an apparently generic *man* to a very clearly androcentric
he, as our examples have shown, why do styleguide writers, teachers
and grammarians continue to prescribe it? Why do editors continue
to defend it? Feminists have argued that arguments in favour of
man, mankind, he and other generic masculine terms cannot be
based on substantive linguistic arguments, but are political. As well
as supporting a male-dominated social order, prescriptive grammar
attempts to legislate against majority usage (for example, by out-
lawing singular *they* as epicene pronoun, as well as non-standard
forms like 'ain't', 'gonna', 'learn' used to mean 'teach' and so on).

In other words, in prescribing rather than describing usage, teachers, grammarians and editors aim to uphold a standard or elite variety of the language which is at odds with the language of most people.

The arguments against androcentric pseudo-generics are varied. Research in psychology does show that thought is affected by language, that mental imagery is different according to whether -*man* suffix/-*person* suffix/no suffix words are used, and that this affects subjects' judgements of the personality attributed to such targets (McConnell and Fazio 1996). The authors review experiments in psychology which test the effects of 'he/man' language upon visual judgements (Wilson and Ng 1988), description of physical characteristics (McConnell and Gavanski 1994), and likelihood to apply for jobs (Bem and Bem 1973). These, and other studies reported on here, demonstrate that sexist language influences the judgement of subjects in such experiments. Of course, all laboratory-type experimentation is subject to a range of criticisms, especially the charge that behaviour is being examined outside the normal context of everyday life. Nonetheless, the consistency of the findings is remarkable, and recent work in cognitive psychology (e.g. Ng 1990) has shown conclusively that *he, man* and *his* are coded in memory as members of the masculine linguistic category. A study comparing a grammatical gender language, Spanish, with English, commonly called a natural gender language, revealed that reading speed was slowed down by 'mismatching' pronouns to agentive antecedents with clearly stereotypical values. (Carreiras *et al.* 1996). Obviously the stereotypes in question derive from world-knowledge, rather than linguistic features, in the case of true epicenes in English (i.e. words without gender markers, such as *journalist, teacher, athlete*). These words then put a lot of pressure on pronouns. Formerly considered to be grammatical words, or function words, rather than lexical words or content words, pronouns are now increasingly being seen as contributing to meaning (Newman 1992).

These studies give the lie to claims that generic *he* is correct and unremarkable, like that of the highly successful Strunk and White guide:

> the use of *he* as pronoun for nouns embracing both genders is a simple, practical convention rooted in the beginnings of the English language. *He* has lost all suggestions of maleness in these circumstances. . . . It has no pejorative connotations; it is never incorrect.

(1979: 60)

While these psychology studies focus on reactions to the use of 'he/man' language, a study by Khosroshahi (1989) compared women's and men's reactions to generic *he*, singular *they* and feminist *he or she* to test their interpretations. She also correlated these interpretations with subjects' own use of generics in written work submitted by them as part of their coursework. On the basis of her evaluation, she categorized students into four groups, women/men who had reformed their language and women/men who used none of the alternatives to pseudo-generic *he*. She found that only women who had reformed their own language reported female imagery as a response to generic *he*. Just as predicted by Nilsen (Nilsen *et al.* 1977), as we saw earlier, men who had reformed their own use of generic pronouns by using *they* or *he or she* still displayed a tendency to imagine male referents in response to generic *he*.

Of the three options tested (*he, they* and *he or she*), the last one, *he or she*, elicited most female imagery. Significantly, it is the only one which specifically names a potential female referent. These findings support the view that he/man language reinforces the invisibility of women. Khosroshahi's results suggest that linguistic behaviour does affect or reflect thought for women who have reformed their language. This supports the weak version of the Sapir–Whorf hypothesis. However, the results of the reformed-language men suggest the opposite: their use of non-sexist language is not mirrored by thinking. She concludes that language reform was initiated by women and works for them, the group who need and benefit from it the most, and explains her results by reference to the distinction between compliance (surface change) and conversion or internalization (modification of values). Thus, changing what we do may change what we think, at least if we benefit from it.

While all the aforementioned writers have focused on generics from the point of view of the concerns of psychology, a large number of articles have appeared with a more linguistic focus. Feminists have studied what Miller and Swift (1976) called 'the pronoun problem' largely in order to encourage reform. They have pointed out that *he* as generic is flawed, often inventing humorous examples to do so, or by quoting actual uses of generic *he* being used to odd effect. Like other writers, Miller and Swift suggest a variety of alternatives, including pluralizing antecedents to agree with a following *they*, using *he or she* instead of the offending *he* or reformulating sentences to avoid any use of the generic, by recasting the thought.

MacKay (1983) argued against generic *he* in an article which became well-known, not for its author's useful arguments against *he*, but for his suggestion that a neologism such as 'E' would in the long term be the best solution. MacKay examines how *he* is used, understood, learned and interpreted in thought. 'Prescriptive' *he*, as he calls it, is not used generically in practice (as we have seen). It is not understood generically, but with male bias, even in generic contexts which should serve to disambiguate this *he* from the sex-specific *he*. On the contrary, *he* used after neutral antecedents such as *person, pedestrian* or *writer* is interpreted as masculine (MacKay 1983: 43). He argues that *he* does not have the semantic flexibility assumed by prescriptive grammarians:

> But the primary meaning of *he* is diametrically opposed to its secondary *he or she* meaning: the primary meaning excludes women whereas the prescribed meaning is intended to include them. Incomparable primary and secondary meanings interfere with one another and a prescription such as '*true* will henceforth and in certain contexts mean *false*' could be expected to be met with a comparable lack of success.

MacKay argues against the claim that the issue of generic *he* is trivial, by referring to evidence that prescriptive *he* may:

> contribute to the feelings of importance, power, and superiority which are common among men, and the feelings of unimportance, powerlessness, and inferiority which are common among women.
> (1983: 48)

In arguing for a neologism, MacKay has to find fault with the so-called singular *they*. He claims it leads to ambiguity of reference, loss of imageability, impact and precision and to problems for its normal plural function. Pateman (1982: 43) argues against an earlier version of MacKay's position on *they*, that 'This problem cannot be reduced from a political to a technical one . . .' In other words, since prescriptive *he* is a political choice it can be countered by prescriptive *they* if the (radical) political will is there.

This whole question of prescribing usage is an interesting but unusual one for linguists nowadays. Prescriptivism is one of linguistics' own 'dirty words', and most linguists pride themselves on the discipline's descriptive ethos. Nonetheless, urging people to retain *he*, to 'legalise' *they* or to change to *he or she* is prescriptive in intent. The focus on the pronoun has resulted partly because of what has been perceived as a gap, an absence, within English. Jespersen himself described the he/man tendency of English to represent a defect in the language (1964 [1924]: 231) and decried the lack of a pronoun to refer to either sex (1894: 27–30). Newman (1992) notes that linguists' views on the subject have hardly changed in decades, although criteria for prescriptive moves have changed from the early concern with logic and analogies with languages like Latin and Greek to today's concerns with gender equality (1992: 447–8). Newman suggests that this so-called 'gap' in English is not a gap at all, since pronouns of a truly epicene type are rare in the world's languages. Faced with ambiguous antecedent nouns, English speakers use world-knowledge in choosing *they, he, he or she,* or occasionally *she* as pick-up pronoun.

Newman counteracts Spender's (1985) and Mühlhäusler and Harré's (1990) argument that **epicene** *he* dates only from the eighteenth or nineteenth century and attests its use as far back as Chaucer's *Canterbury Tales* (Newman 1992: 448–9), though he accepts that standardization led to the opting for *he* as default pronoun in English. His own data (uses of epicene pronominals used by TV chat show guests) support the claims of earlier writers such as Bodine (1975) that, in speech at least, singular *they* is the most common epicene in English (Newman 1992: 460). Moreover, he notes that when it is used, it does not result necessarily from a speaker's desire to avoid making a commitment to gender. Thus, he quotes a speaker who uses *one* followed by *their husband,* where obviously the person with a husband is a woman. In other words, *they* used as a singular, has effects/uses other than those identified as relevant by feminists, including potential reference to notional plurality. It is precisely its ambiguity – or ability to refer to one or many – which makes it the pronoun of choice. *They* can also work to make the referent more 'fuzzy', or less identifiable. So, it hides identity, or de-solidifies the referent, rather than just including both genders (Newman 1992: 467).

The choice of epicene *they* is discussed in great detail, with many examples, in Meyer (1993). The article addresses the history of epicene *they,* resistance to its use, current use and meanings, and lists a range of 'masters (sic) of the language' such as Congreve, George Eliot, Shelley, Austen, Shaw, Shakespeare and Cardinal Newman who used it frequently (Meyers 1993: 183–4). The conclusion drawn is that singular *they* offers the greatest challenge to generic masculine *he.*

Although the focus here has been on *man* and *he, he/man* language extends to a far greater range of terms than these two. Nilsen examined one dictionary and found an overall ratio of three masculine words to one feminine word (Nilsen *et al.* 1977: 34). When the words denoted skill or power, the ratio shifted to 6:1, but when they carried negative connotations the ratio was reversed: 25 feminine words to 20 masculine. Similarly, words marking age are skewed towards women, showing that a woman's age matters more than a man's in male-dominated societies where men usually seek to marry and to employ women who are younger, less experienced and less powerful than themselves.

Removing the suffix -*man* or replacing it with -*person* does not always work, such are the pervasiveness and productivity of this small word. The feminist coinage *chairperson* has been resisted very strongly, especially in the US, and, when used, has tended to be used just for women, leaving *chairman* intact. Resistance to new, neutral generics and feminist coinages such as *Ms* can be viewed as an indicator of our culture's desire to mark gender and women's sexual availability. It is sobering to read Nilsen's list of 80 terms containing the item *man* (Nilsen *et al.* 1977: 36) if one has pretensions to help effect language reform of a gender-inclusive kind. Included are nouns like *baseman, countryman, forefather, middleman*; compounds such as *workmen's compensation, one-man show*; verbs like *to patronize* or *to fraternize,* and adjectives such as *statesmanlike, sportsmanlike* and *masterful.* Are women meant to feel included in the *brotherhood of man?* Can we be trusted to be a *man of his word?* Are we capable of a *masterstroke,* a *masterpiece* or of making a *gentleman's agreement?* Although anti-feminists, such as William Safire, and some feminists have argued that the issue of language is trivial compared to the issue of, say, equal rights or equal pay, we should not forget that rights are enshrined in law by means of language.

Effects of androcentric language on society

A great deal of law involves the interpretation of statutes and women's rights have been dependent historically upon the interpretation given to such legal language. Sachs and Hoff Wilson (1978) show how in Britain, Canada and the US, women fought battles over such language. The rights of women to study and practice medicine, to own property, to vote and to stand for election have all hinged upon the interpretation of generic, supposedly neutral terms like *citizen* and *person.* Are women *persons?* was the central issue in deciding whether women would be admitted to study and graduate from the University of Edinburgh medical school in the late 1860s. 'Words importing the masculine gender should be deemed and taken to include females' according to the 1850 British statute for reducing the length of written Acts. Thus, women claimed they could vote in Manchester in 1869, because 'every man of full age' should, logically, include women. Twenty years later Lady Sandhurst won an election to the London County Council by a clear majority, but her (male) opponent had her election declared void because, as a woman, she could not come within the expression 'fit person of full age' (Sachs and Hoff Wilson 1978: 25).

Other strong arguments against the pernicious effects of sexist language concern teaching materials for schools and universities. Nilsen (Nilsen *et al.* 1977) discusses at some length the effects of a reading programme, Alpha One, aimed at infants, in which the consonants of English were described as boys and vowels as girls. Inevitably, the vowels were portrayed as weak, dependent and generally stereotypically feminine and the consonants as boisterous, fun-loving and adventurous. A follow-up evaluation of the reading programme by a graduate student in reading concluded of the Alpha One system:

> There was a direct correlation ... between the length of exposure to the Alpha One program and the degree to which the children identified activities as belonging in the male and female domains as stereotyped in the Alpha One program.
>
> (Nilsen, in Nilsen *et al.* 1977: 168)

Other studies, including very recent ones, show continued marginalization of girls and women and stereotypical portrayals bearing little resemblance to current social and demographic trends. Language is central to these portrayals, and no discipline seems exempt, whether it be English as a foreign language (Hellinger 1980), law (Kurzon 1989), business (Nielsen 1988), maths (Sherman 1983), economics (Polanyi and Strassmann 1993) or even linguistics. Macaulay and Brice (1997) show how, despite guidelines to counter sexism in language, current textbooks in syntax are replete with stereotypical examples and imbalance in the number of sentences referring to women and men. Males are given occupations five times more often than females and the occupations are highly stereotyped. Males are far more likely to be called a 'genius', 'intelligent' or 'brilliant' and women are more likely to be identified as someone's wife than men as someone's husband, and more likely to be described in terms of physical appearance. The authors do not claim that such sexist sentences are only found in textbooks by male authors. They do argue that exposure to sexism in textbooks is a significant problem, as it can lead to lowering of performance, altered perceptions of the suitability of careers, and the creation of a 'chilly climate' in the chosen field (Macaulay and Brice 1997: 820). Saeed's (1997) *Semantics* offers an amusing corrective to such texts. Marginalization of women and girls in classroom materials is also reinforced, often unwittingly, by teachers' behaviour in mixed classes, where boys seek and achieve a disproportionate amount of the teacher's attention, if only by being disruptive or obstreperous (Sarah 1980).

Inscribing women's meanings in language

These examples have been explored in order to point out how **androcentrism** in language reflects masculist social meaning. If such language inscribes men's meanings, presumably women's own coinages and use of language will inscribe women's meanings. What would become of women's authentic words in a culture which marginalizes women? Would women's verbal inventions radically alter a sexist society accustomed to viewing and describing social realities from men's point of view? Would women's words 'stick' or would they be lost? Perhaps they would change, as so many words do over time. After all, etymology has shown us that words and their meanings do not enjoy a permanent relationship. They die out, are borrowed and reborrowed, are legislated for, and against, are invented or lost. Legislating for or against words does not often work, as successive French ministers of culture have found in their attempts to stem borrowing from English into their language. While they may exercise, as do editors and lexicographers, some control over spelling and the written language, speech is notoriously difficult to influence. People resist interference with their speech habits. It is not difficult to imagine that conservative and anti-feminist men (and women) would resist feminist linguistic proposals which challenge their views. Word choice does reflect ideology or political position. One woman's terrorist is another's freedom fighter and many successful feminist slogans use language to draw attention to women's alternative views of patriarchal society:

When God made Man, she made a mistake.

When feminists coin words to express feminist ideas and perceptions the hope is that social change will ensue. The point of altering professional titles to be gender inclusive was to break down the stereotype which associated such terms and such jobs with men only, thus widening the range of job opportunities for women. As we saw, gender-inclusive job advertising does lead to more female applicants. As a preliminary caution to the outline on feminist lexical inventions, we should note that many feminists consider that changing the language is a necessary but insufficient move in changing an androcentric world order. Changing language is inadequate to alter the material processes and social structures which keep women subordinate (Cameron 1985, Black and Coward 1990, Graddol and Swann 1989, McConnell-Ginet 1989). To take up the job vacancy advertisement example again, altering the wording of such ads does not guarantee that a woman will be called for interview, selected, employed, promoted or given equal pay, even if more women do apply. Even legislation for equal opportunities has not been able to effect such change, so it is highly doubtful that language could ever do so. Opening up male-dominated employment sectors to women has required a lot more than linguistic tampering. Feminists have challenged stereotyping in education and training, promotion, in families and have sought to secure legislation against various forms of discrimination, and to raise the consciousness of male trade unionists to do so. To argue that language reform is trivial compared to these other struggles is to miss the point. Language is the vehicle for the other forms of discrimination: Women cannot be full members of many working*men*'s clubs. Women are not always 'men' or *persons* and much of the work women do, is somehow not 'work'. A 1970s campaign for wages for housework was effective in launching a major debate in left-wing political circles by putting the 'work' back in 'housework', and constructing housewives/'homemakers' as workers.

Around the same time, a number of feminists began to write feminist dictionaries to re-define meanings given by men and to chart the emergence of women's meanings and coinages. In their preface to *A Feminist Dictionary*, Kramarae and Treichler describe their aims as:

> to document words, definitions, and conceptualizations that
> illustrate women's linguistic contributions; to illuminate forms

of expression through which women have sought to describe, reflect upon, and theorize about women, language, and the world; to identify issues of language theory, research, usage, and institutionalized practice that bear on the relationship between women and language; to demonstrate ways in which women are seizing the language; to broaden knowledge of the feminist lexicon; and to stimulate research on women and language.

(1985: 1)

One of the main reasons for writing a feminist dictionary is to correct the omissions and distortions of traditional (malestream) lexicographers. Gershuny's Ph.D. study (1973), an examination of the Random House Dictionary, shows how sexism can appear in the invented sentences used to illustrate a term in context, a finding similar to that already noted in relation to sample sentences in textbooks of syntax (Macaulay and Brice 1997). Gershuny found that references to men outnumbered those to women by 3:1, and that stereotyping was evident at many levels of linguistic analysis (lexicon, agency, transitivity). Dictionaries may also omit or distort women's meanings by what Morris (1982) calls 'code control'. Her example, cited in Kramarae and Treichler (1985: 2) is of the Australian Macquarie Dictionary's entry for the words *sexism* and *sexist*. *Sexism* is defined as 'the upholding or propagation of sexist attitudes'. A 'sexist attitude' is one which 'stereotypes a person according to gender or sexual preference'. No doubt women are persons as far as that sentence is concerned! These definitions of *sexism* and *sexist* dilute feminist meanings. Sexism is not just about attitudes, but about material practices (such as womanslaughter, woman-battering, rape, pornography, child abuse, prostitution, genital mutilation, exclusion from rights, from religious office, and so on). It was feminists who invented the term to refer to the treatment of women, not of generic *persons*. Women may hold anti-male 'attitudes' but we do not have the power to translate them into a range of anti-male practices. The Macquarie Dictionary glosses over the material aspects of sexism, and renders it a problem for men as well as women. To outline the difference, let us remember the apocryphal claim that when asked what they feared most from women, men said 'that they'll laugh at us'. Women asked the same question about men replied 'that they'll kill us'.

Kramarae and Treichler's dictionary (1985) re-defines many words we already know the meaning of (like *marriage, man-made, Marilyn Monroe*), but, by giving contextual fragments from feminist writers to illustrate the terms, provide an almost encyclopaedic view of the world from an alternative perspective. They also include many feminist coinages, such as *man-junky, fairytale brigade, pink pig award* and *ogle-in*, and commentaries, rather than definitions of key terms. There are also extracts from women's poetry used to flesh out definitions. My favourite comes under the entry for *vagina* which I quote here to give the reader the flavour of this intriguing, highly browsable text:

> A famous poet told me, 'Vagina's ugly'.
> Meaning of course, the sound of it. In
>   poems.
> Meanwhile, he inserts his penis frequently
> into his verse, calling it seriously, 'My Penis'.
> It is short, I know, and dignified.
> I mean of course the sound of it. In
>   poems.
>   (Joan Larkin 1975: 59 in Kramarae and Treicher 1985: 468)

Another entry of interest is that for *reclamation* defined as 'feminist linguistic process in which individual words and concepts, given negative meanings through patriarchal traditions and writings, are identified, examined, re-defined, and thus reclaimed' (Kramarae and Treichler 1985: 386). An early French feminist journal *Sorcières* (witches) used this strategy, common to many international feminist groups. Words such as *dyke, bitch* and *shrew* have been used with positive connotations by feminists. Young African Americans have begun to use the term 'nigga' as an in-group word and thirty years ago, the slogan 'Black is Beautiful' aimed at a similar reclamation. When straight people became comfortable with *gay* and *lesbian*, *queer* was revived for reclamation. An element in reclamation then appears to be a desire for an in-group vocabulary to assert positive meanings for the group. Few liberal whites or heterosexuals, I would argue, are (yet) happy to use *nigga* or *queer* although racist homophobes have probably never stopped using them. In a sense this shows that dictionaries are limited. Words do not exist in a vacuum, but always in a context and contexts are socially, culturally, economically, aesthetically, politically and historically determined.

Thus, groups who reclaim words are exercising a kind of power. The most famed feminist exponent of reclaiming is American philosopher-theologian Mary Daly, whose feminist re-workings of words often involve no more than hyphenating them to draw attention to their separate morphemes and thus remind readers of the words' actual etymologies, or sometimes, of fictive ones. Thus *being* is spelled *be-ing* and *therapist* is spelled *the/rapist* (Daly 1978:

24n), the latter presumably as an attack on psychiatry, a discipline many feminists view, along with gynaecology, as the ultimate in androcentrism and misogyny.

Another approach to the disruption of language and meaning is that of Elgin, inventor of a feminist language called Láadan, in which she wrote a novel, *Native Tongue* (1985), with an added glossary. Elgin went perhaps further than other feminists by pointing up the inadequacy of what others had viewed as man-made, or androcentric language, by filling in a huge number of 'lexical gaps'. The lexical gap is a notion derived from translation, referring to a specific translation problem, common in translating across language pairs from very different cultures. The Japanese expression, *naijo no ko*, glossed roughly as 'success from outside help' refers to the business success of a Japanese man resulting from the aid and sacrifices of his wife (Cherry 1991: 64). The nearest equivalent notion is the English saying: 'Behind every successful man is a woman.' Elgin's work fills the lexical gaps found in translating from man-made English into woman-made Láadan. Cameron's reader in the feminist critique of language (1990) contains an extract from a *First Dictionary and Grammar of Láadan*, the glossary from *Native Tongue*. I particularly like *radama* which means to 'non-touch, to actively refrain from touching', and *radamalh*, to 'non-touch with evil intent'. Another pair of verbs I believe feminist linguists working on conversational analysis (see Chapter 6) might find useful are *ramime*, 'to refrain from asking, out of courtesy and kindness', and *ramimelh*, 'to refrain from asking, with evil intent, especially when it is clear that someone wants the other to ask' (Elgin in Cameron 1990: 162–3).

As far as I'm aware these words have not really caught on, and feminists appropriating Daly's hyphenation techniques are few and far between outside university departments in Anglophone countries. Re-workings such as Daly's, or those of French and Canadian feminist writers such as Cixous, Brossard, Wittig and Irigaray are notoriously difficult to translate, precisely because their techniques involve the alteration of words to pinpoint alternative and plural meanings (Simon 1996). However, there *are* feminist coinages which have caught on, words which attempt to inscribe women's meanings and interpretations. It is to their fate we turn now.

Feminist coinages have been opposed and challenged in the home, in universities, at work, and, crucially in the press. Ehrlich and King (1994) examine their fate to see how such innovations are appropriated by the speech community at large. They examine two kinds of words: (a) those which aim to replace an existing sexist term, and (b) those which aim to fill a lexical gap. Even if such words fail, or are re-appropriated, the feminist critique of language encapsulated in the innovation has the merit of raising people's awareness of the issues and exposing androcentric perspectives (1994: 61).

Under the first category of words, Ehrlich and King examine replacements for generic masculine words, which we have already discussed. It is the second category which is of particular interest, those linguistic innovations which aim to name women's experiences. These are terms like *sexism* (already mentioned in relation to the Macquarie dictionary definition), *sexual harassment, feminism, date rape, macho* and *phallocentric*. They note that introducing new terms is not enough. Language, or the control of meanings, is an on-going struggle, and the meanings feminists intend may not always prevail. Like any other words, they may not be appropriated as hoped by their coiners. The form of address, *Ms,* and the term *gender* as used in feminist theory, are two good examples of such misappropriation. *Ms* was intended to replace *Miss* and *Mrs* but has, in practice, often been added to them. For many it is used for a woman whose marital status is in doubt, or for a separated, divorced or cohabiting woman. While the original impetus was to stop naming women in terms of their relationship to men, for such users, *Ms* has become a handy label for women in an in-between state. Others do, of course, use it as if it were an insult, connoting 'feminist' or 'lesbian' to them. The fate of the word *gender* is similar, as it now often replaces *sex* while feminists set the concept against sex, understood as given, to mark gender as socially constructed (Delphy 1984: 144). This distinction between given but meaningless anatomical sex and gender is lost when *gender* is used instead of *sex*.

Ehrlich and King focus on news reporting in the press and outline strategies used by a sexist press to limit and distort feminist meaning. These strategies involve re-definition, expansion *ad absurdum* of the content or denotation of the term in order to trivialize it, suggestions that the phenomenon named does not actually exist by using quotation marks or other metalinguistic markers (such as 'so-called date-rape'), and other, similar tactics. An analogy is drawn with new terms intended to challenge racist language and ethnic slurs.

The general conclusion of this useful paper is that definition is a site of ideological struggle. Sexist language does not only reflect sexist realities, it also helps to reproduce them. One valuable result of feminist, anti-racist and anti-homophobic linguistic innovation is that the pejorative words they seek to replace are no longer unmarked or neutral. While constant use of *he or she* and *her or his* mark people off as at least nominally aware of, and sympathetic to, feminist ideals, the continued use of prescriptive *he* and generic masculine terms now marks the user's language as unreformed. In a counter-argument to Spender's call for encoding women into language, Black and Coward (1990) make the point that generic masculine language actually fails to encode men, that is as men, as specific, historically situated people and not the norm:

> The discursive formation which allows men to represent themselves as non-gendered and to define women constantly according to their sexual status is a discursive formation with very definite effects. It allows men to deny the effect of their gendered subjectivity on women. It is not a question of men secretly believing that masculine is the norm. What is available to them is a discourse where gender and sexual identity seem to be absent. . . . Our aim is not just to validate the new meanings of women but to confront men with their maleness. This is not just about masculine behaviour, but about discursive practices. It is about making men take responsibility for being men. Men are sustained at the centre of the stage precisely because they can be 'people' and do not have to represent their masculinity to themselves. They never need see themselves or their maleness as a problem.
>
> (1990: 132)

Summary

- underneath language reform proposals is the belief that language reflects or determines social structures, thought and perception

- cross-cultural studies show that a language reflects the needs of its speakers and the culture they inhabit

- there is no consensus among feminists regarding the question of the relationship between language and culture

- generic masculine terms have been shown empirically not to work, and women and men appear not to use them the same way

- language reform does not always work as intended: generics may still conjure up male referents; feminist coinages may be used contrary to intention

- meaning is never given, but always a site of struggle among users

Further reading

Spender, Dale 1985 *Man-made language* (2nd edition) Routledge and Kegan Paul, London, Chapter 5.

Nilsen, Alleen P. *et al.* 1977 *Sexism and Language*, National Council of Teachers of English, Urbana, Illinois, Chapter 2.

Kramarae, Cheris and Treichler, Paula A. 1985 *A feminist dictionary*, Pandora Press, London, 'Introduction: Words on a feminist dictionary', pp. 1–22.

Ehrlich, Susan and King, Ruth 1994 'Feminist meanings and the depoliticization of the lexicon', in *Language in society*, 23: 59–76.

Martyna, Wendy 1980 'The Psychology of the generic masculine', in McConnell-Ginet Sally *et al.* (eds) 1980 *Women and language in literature and society*, Praeger, New York, Chapter 5, pp. 69–79.

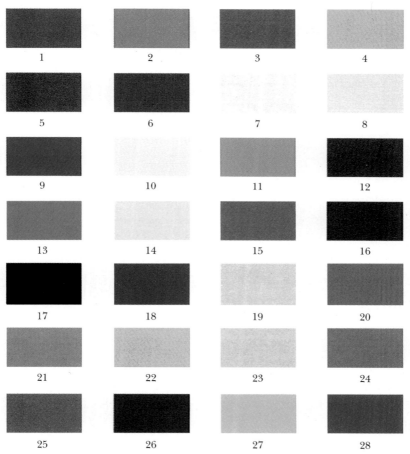

Exercise on Gouro colour terms

Chapter 4

Gender in the English language: an exploration

Chapter outline

This chapter will provide a close investigation of English from the perspective of gender, with a focus on lexis (vocabulary) and grammar. The aims of this chapter are:

- to raise readers' awareness of language
- to examine how women and men are described and addressed in the language
- to explore the question of the relationship between language and social reality

These topics will be examined by focusing on a variety of separate features, and these provide the sub-divisions of the chapters, namely

- naming analysis
- collocation
- the vocabulary of insults and swearing
- politically correct language
- names of professions and occupations

Naming analysis

In this section we will examine the question of how we name and address people (**onomastics**, titles, forms of address) and how we name social relationships.

Onomastics

In the film *The English Patient*, the protagonist Count Álmasy is suffering from partial amnesia. A former ally who believes the Count has betrayed him wishes to find out if the patient, severely disfigured and unrecognizable, really is the man he suspects him to be. He doubts that the Count has lost his memory and asserts 'you never forget your own name'. In a sense, the name is synonymous with the self.

Names are important in all human cultures. Language defines us as a species and our individual names, usually given in ritual ceremonies, and sometimes altered in further ceremonies representing rites of passage, label us as separate beings. Giving names to people and to things is a kind of power: in hierarchical social arrangements, it is the more powerful who determine the rules of naming. Parents name children, teachers determine how they will call pupils but pupils are told what to call teachers. Equally banal is the practice of some male mechanics who call female clients 'love' or 'pet'. Feminists such as Spender have argued that the right to name brings with it the power to define the named. Later in this chapter, I will apply this argument to a discussion of the language surrounding prostitution and surrogate motherhood.

Reference sections in bookshops invariably contain a number of books listing names for children. Always, the list is divided into two: names for girls and names for boys (though not in that order usually!). Parents-to-be often discuss names for months, prefacing every suggestion with 'if it's a girl . . .' or 'if it's a boy . . .'. Odd though it may seem, one's given name affects how a person will be viewed by others. Names, like other words, carry connotations and we do not expect the same things of a 'Margaret', a 'Sue-Ellen', a 'Babs' or a 'Gertrude', nor of a 'Calvin', a 'Percival', an 'Abraham' or a 'Pete'. More obviously, we do not expect the same of a Patrick and a Patricia. Names follow fashions; they have religious, regional, period and class connotations. In ethnically divided and sectarian societies, one's name may be sufficient to set a person up for a beating. One writer on names wonders if girls' names will reflect the feminist aspirations of their mothers (Lieberson 1984).

Many people deliberately change their names to reflect an awareness of an emerging identity, a crisis, a change in religious affiliation and so on. Cassius Clay/Mohammed Ali is one famous example. Bass and Davis in *The Power To Heal* (1990) point out that sexual abuse survivors may find it useful to change their names as part of the recovery process. A number of feminists, in particular lesbian feminists, have opted to lose their inherited patronymic surname, adopting for example a foremother's given name as a new surname. Two well-known feminist linguists, Kramarae and Penelope, have deliberately changed their names. Far more commonly, however, women change their names in ways many feminists find unacceptable: on marriage. Western women have objected to this practice for a long time. Unfortunately, what women do and say is easily rendered invisible, so each generation seems to be attacked anew for rocking the boat. When women in the 1960s, 1970s and since refused to take their husbands' names upon marriage, many objected as if this refusal were a shocking new idea. Earlier, nineteenth-century feminists had fought for the right not to change to or append a husband's surname (Frank and Anshen 1983: 11).

Resistance comes from many quarters. While male tennis players are called by their surname at Wimbledon, women are referred to by surname and a title to indicate marital status. If named, they are referred to by their husband's surname, even if such is not their choice, and there is something faintly ridiculous about referring to out-of-the-closet lesbian athletes as 'Miss'. The resistance to women claiming the right to name themselves and to use a title which does not indicate marital status, reflects resistance to women's attempts to alter traditional understandings of women's roles within and outside marriage.

One of the most important things a name does, then, is to mark gender. One baby-naming book specifically recommends parents to choose a name that identifies the child's sex. Names which can be used for either sex are rare and usually marked for sex by different spellings, e.g. Lesley/Leslie. Once a name is used for girls, it loses popularity as a boy's name, e.g. Beverley, Gayle, Evelyn, Shirley. Research has shown that boys' names differ phonologically from girls, being shorter and ending frequently in a stop (p,t,k etc.) In cultures using Indo-European languages, girls' names are often derivatives of boys', and formed by Latinate suffixes which lengthen the name, often adding a vowel ending, e.g. Roberta, Henrietta, Patricia. While many boys' names in English have no immediately obvious meaning, women are often named after virtues considered suitable such as Patience or Faith, after precious stones (Ruby) or flowers (Violet, Lily). If one's name <u>does</u> affect how one is perceived by others and therefore one's life chances, it could be a liability to be named after a rather insignificant, minuscule flower. Maximilian may have more opportunities than Daisy.

Titles and forms of address

We have already seen how feminists have attempted to equalize the treatment of women and men by coining *Ms*. This new title was intended to replace *Miss* and *Mrs* so all women could be referred to without drawing attention to marital status, as men are with *Mr*. Resistance to *Ms* has taken many forms, including outright refusal to use it. In practice, what has happened is that it has been added to *Miss* and *Mrs* in many cases. By some, it is seen as useful until one has ascertained whether the *Ms* in question is a *Miss* or a *Mrs*. Others seem to think it refers to divorcees and separated women and/or to lesbians and/or feminists.

While not totally successful then, *Ms* does allow women who choose it, to use a title which gives them the privacy men take for granted. Moreover, as Cameron points out in *Verbal Hygiene* (1995) its very existence as an option marks non-users' choice of *Miss/Mrs* as the choice it is. More of this under political correctness later in this chapter.

In other countries, where marital status is marked by title for women but not men, feminists have reacted differently. In Germany, for example, *Fräulein* (Miss) is no longer used and all women are referred to as *Frau* (formerly Mrs). By law in France, unmarried mothers are to be referred to as *Madame*, and it is considered impolite to address an unknown woman as anything but *Madame*. *Mademoiselle* may, then, be going the same way as *Fräulein*.

Resistance from men may well stem from a lack of imagination about the issue. Perhaps if women insisted on asking unknown men 'is that *Mr* or *Master*?' when introduced, men would have more happily espoused the new title proposed for women.

Other objections raised by feminists include the unreciprocated use of titles, of surnames and of first names. While many languages make a distinction between intimates and non-intimates by the use of different pronouns (called the T/V distinction after the *tu/vous* type pronouns in most European languages), English relies on terms of address to do this. As mentioned earlier, teachers will normally be called by title plus surname, while pupils are called by first name (if girls) and first or surname if boys. Reciprocal use of nicknames marks an intra-generational community while pet names mark the most intimate relationships and may be secret. A glance at national newspaper small-ads on St. Valentine's day will provide a good sample, and could be used for a simple exercise: check for agreement among class-mates on the gender of 'your big huggy bear' and 'my sweet sugar-dumpling' (see Langford 1997 for a discussion).

One reason feminists have fought for the right to name ourselves is that women are often on the down side of non-reciprocated usage. In offices, for example, men may be referred to by title and surname and women by first name or a diminutive. I once witnessed a telling example at a promotional breakfast for language graduands. Students organizing the events prepared name tags for their lecturers. All the women's tags bore first name and surname (e.g. I was 'Maggie Gibbon, staff'), while all the men's bore title, initial and surname. The students were all female. When challenged, incidentally, no disrespect had been intended: in fact, the students claimed to feel closer to their women lecturers and to view the titles as a form of distancing. They claimed women staff rarely used them themselves, while the men did. My concern, and that of my colleagues, was that these young women were indirectly selling themselves short to the business people invited by undermining the achievements of other women. A similar practice was common during the 1970s. At my university, the internal telephone directory listed all the men by surname and initial and all the women by surname, first name and title. In the case of academic women, they were stripped of their doctorates or professorships and listed as *Miss* or *Mrs.* A few years later, the women's academic titles were used but their marital status added in brackets. In this instance, as in others, we shall discuss how feminists ask for parity, not separate or different status. Using initials for men and given names for women serves the function of marking the two as different. The fate of the coinage *Ms* and of words like *chairperson, congressperson* to refer only to women, with *chairman* etc. referring to men, instead of being used for either sex as desired by feminists, shows that, in our culture, the marking of gender seems crucial. Why this should be can only be understood by reference to feminist theories.

Naming relationships

It is a commonplace of relativist thinking in linguistics to draw attention to kinship terms in different cultures to show how languages differ in how they 'divide up' or categorize reality. We saw, for example, how in Japan where age is is more salient than in the West and honour is due to elders, sisters and brothers have different terms according to whether they are younger or older. While we have one word, *uncle,* for a father's or mother's brother or brother-in-law, some cultures have words to specify whether it is a maternal or paternal uncle we are referring to. The existence of different terms suggests that the meaning of each is different, as few languages can afford the luxury of true synonyms. Perhaps in such a culture, the social relationship between a person and their maternal uncle is constrained or built up according to different rules, rights, obligations and expectations from those applying in the case of a paternal uncle. Perhaps one of these uncles plays the role that godparents once played in Western societies and still do in some, particularly South European Catholic societies. So it appears that we name what is salient or important to us in our culture. Westerners do not name our uncles differently because the niece–uncle relationship does not alter according to which side of the family the uncle is on.

Feminists have explored this idea of naming what is important and not naming what is not to draw attention to sexist aspects of our own culture. Sara Mills (1995), for example, has written on the lack of neutral or positive words for women to use about our own genitalia. We have either negative, slang or swear words, or else euphemistic terms, or again Greek- or Latin-derived medical terms. Elgin in Cameron (1990: 162) has 'invented' a feminist lexicon to fill such lexical gaps, and in creating words, given recognition to unsayable feelings and anger. The example of *radíidin* springs to mind. This word means something like 'unholiday', an occasion meant to be a holiday but which, for women, is not one. As Elgin says, there are too many guests and none of them help. Mills comments that the verb 'to nag' tends to take a female subject (wife) and a male object (husband), yet we have no word for a man who refuses to do his share of housework and therefore gets 'nagged', i.e. asked repeatedly to do so in the face of his refusal! An interesting counter example of a plethora of terms is provided by Cameron (1992a). Students in a class experiment were asked to come up with all the terms they could find for 'penis'. Over a hundred, mostly positive, were listed.

In my own research on reproductive technology and related issues, I have been struck by the existence of lexical gaps. I would like here to focus on two areas which I think are more obviously related than may appear: prostitution and surrogate motherhood.

As a preliminary exercise, I suggest you try writing down a list, giving yourself three minutes each time, of all the names you can think of for people involved in prostitution and in surrogate motherhood. Then I suggest you look up *prostitution* and related terms like *prostitute* and *surrogate* and *mother* in a recent dictionary, preferably a corpus-based dictionary which gives the words with contextual information, showing how the word is commonly used. Then try the same with a thesaurus, or if you have access to it, use the British National Corpus.

What you will probably find are certain lexical gaps. These two concepts, prostitution and surrogacy, provide us with excellent examples of the relationship between a culture and the words used within that culture to serve its speakers. What interests me here is what a language *can* say, what a language *cannot* say and what a language must say or cannot avoid saying. *Prostitution* is a noun. This banal fact covers a multitude of interesting facts about the English language. What do nouns do? How do they work in language? A number of linguists with an interest in language and power (Fairclough 1992, Kress and Hodge 1979, Halliday, in Halliday and Hasan 1989) have written extensively on issues such as this, as we saw in Chapter 2. Feminist thinkers have developed their insights. Nouns like *prostitution* can be termed nominalizations. Most nouns ending in '-tion' fit into this category. Nominalizations are nouns which derive from another part of speech, usually a verb. *Prostitution* is thus the noun form of the verb to *prostitute*, or more likely, of the reflexive verb to *prostitute oneself.* Whereas verbs generally operate in sentences to show processes, nouns – and here I am speaking of nominalizations – come to suggest not a process but a thing, an essence. My feminist contention here is that using nominalized forms allows a few interesting disappearing tricks. The following schema might make this clearer:

Table 4.1 Linguistic disappearing tricks

Noun (Agent)	Verb	Noun (Patient)	Nominalization
hunter	hunts	the hunted	hunt/hunting
surgeon	operates	patient	operation/surgery
?	uses? engages?		
?	prostitutes?	prostitute	prostitution
?	employs?		
prostitute	prostitutes herself/ himself		prostitution
	?	?	surrogacy/ surrogate motherhood
surrogate (mother)	mothers?	baby/foetus	
	carries?		
?	engages?	surrogate/mother	surrogate motherhood

We find it difficult to fill in this schema. Now Kress and Hodge (1979) have argued that reality consists of people doing things which have effects. People do things to people, verbs carry the meaning of such actions or processes. Nouns reify (make into a thing) the process that the verb carries. The point here is that a verb has a subject: we know who is doing the action. Transitive verbs have an object too, so we know to whom or what the subject did that action.

Nominalized forms like 'prostitution' and 'surrogacy' make certain actors disappear. Ask yourself what picture, what person comes to mind when you hear 'prostitution', 'surrogate motherhood'. My guess is you see a 'prostitute', a woman working in prostitution and a 'surrogate mother', a woman carrying a child for others. But prostitution and surrogacy are meant to stand for relations and actions, not just single actors. Both prostitution and surrogacy involve transactions. There are at least two and usually more, persons involved.

Prostitute	'client(s)'	pimp	state/ police/ social workers
Surrogate mother	biological father adoptive mother (commissioning parents)	child	agency lawyers doctors psychiatrists

A close analysis of the words will show that some have very negative connotations and others neutral or positive ones. Some terms are erroneous. Surrogate means 'substitute' or 'stand-in' mother, suggesting this person is not the real mother of the child she bears. 'Client' is a neutral term which can be used for men or women who avail of any service. In the case of prostitution, whether of women or young men, the 'client' appears to be availing of a service, and is deemed morally neutral, while the prostitute (whore, hooker) carries in her name all society's opprobrium. Similarly, negative feelings towards surrogacy are loaded on to the woman desperate enough to sell or rent her womb or her procreative power. In the worst cases, she is even considered to be an exploiter of desperate childless couples. Feminist critiques of both practices abound (Corea 1988, Chesler 1990, Arditti *et al.* 1984). What concerns us though is how language can limit our ability to examine such practices. It is not true that we *cannot* think negatively of the client of prostitution: language does not control our thought to that extent. However, it is *harder* to re-examine our taken-for-granted beliefs when words fail us.

Resistance to feminist coinages like *Ms, chairperson, sexism, sexual harassment, date rape* and *male chauvinist* shows that what is being resisted is women's right to name the world as we see it, as if we matter, as if our experience matters. Feminist renaming makes women visible. Centuries of prescriptivism have tended to make us disappear, as our discussion of *he* showed.

Collocation

Like other languages, English is governed by rules. There is a particular set of rules which are not strictly speaking taught to children learning the language, nor to foreign learners. I refer to rules of collocational constraint. **Collocation** is the term linguists use to talk about which words go with what. The reason I cannot say:

> * Went boy the girl dance over to asked and him the to

is that the order words come in is important. We do not begin declarative sentences in English with verbs but with subjects:

> The girl went over to the boy and asked him to dance.

This is a syntactic constraint: a restriction on word order. Not all languages work like English. Irish and Welsh, for example, do start sentences with the verbs, then put the subject. English sometimes does this too, as when asking a question: 'Are you really Elvis Presley?' Collocational constraint is somewhat different and relates to limits put on the company words can keep, to use a common metaphor. We can say:

> The tired girls slept peacefully

but not:

> The yellow balloons slept peacefully

or:

> The yellow girls slept furiously.

Balloons do not sleep, girls are not yellow and we cannot sleep furiously. These verbal habits limit what we can say and possibly, on a daily basis, do limit how we think. Children sometimes inadvertently create unusual collocations which may strike us as poetic and poets also, deliberately, associate things not usually associated in order to wake readers out of our linguistic and mental straitjackets and to make us see things in a new or startling way.

So far, there does not seem to be much scope for feminist critique here. However, if we examine our language carefully, we will find that there are many ways in which collocation works to create limits to the depiction of women and of men, to reinforce stereotypes and to lull users into lazy and unthinking linguistic ruts.

Feminist discourse analysis is a newly emerging area which focuses on collocation, among other things. This field of research is likely to be opened up by the development of corpus linguistics which permits analysts access to vast corpora of naturally occurring language and which provides tools for searching, selecting, counting and contextualing any string the researcher may wish to check on. Even without technology and using nothing but native-speaker competence and introspection, we can work out that adjectives, to take an example, do not collocate equally with female and male referents. The adjectives 'nagging', 'pretty', 'forceful', 'confident', 'whinging' and 'grubby' are not likely to be applied equally to the nouns 'woman', 'man' and 'child'. Clearly in some way, the adjective 'pretty' contains part of the meaning of the nouns it modifies. We think of 'girl' and 'young woman' as the most likely candidates to be paired with it. If we place 'boy' with 'pretty', most likely we will think of a parrot or a budgie. A 'pretty man' strikes us as odd. Dictionaries do not give us this information explicitly, we come to know it (Gershuny 1973). Appropriate (to our culture) collocation is partly what limits our thought to well-tried formulae. Dictionaries, by their examples, offer an out-dated, sexist view of women and men.

Proverbs, popular quotations and stock phrases do the same. While the many hundreds of sayings using *man* make women invisible, others naturalize what is a cultural arrangement: 'A woman's work is never done.' 'A woman's place is in the home.' Many such sayings, interestingly enough, act as injunctions to women to be silent: 'Hell hath no fury like a woman's scorn.' 'Quand femme il y a, silence il n'y a' (when a woman is present, silence is absent).

Feminists in recent years have begun to look at collocation from the point of view of the construction of agency as predominantly male. For example, the sexual double standard which enjoins men to be active, even predatory, in their pursuit of (heterosexual) sex, encourages women to be reticent, passive or chaste. This double standard is reflected in accounts of sexual encounters in literature, both classic and popular. Feminist discourse analysis in this area has shown how a close investigation of subject and verb choices, and the use of active or passive constructions, can portray women as mere responders to men's sexual advances. In other words, women have often been portrayed as objects of desire, rather than desiring subjects in our own right. Thus, rather than being depicted as subjects in texts, and thus as performing actions, affecting material reality by their actions and intending such effects, female characters are often portrayed as being affected by others' actions (especially those of males) and of colluding in this. Romantic or sexual scenes in books are a very useful source to analyse how language, in particular the collocation of female and male subjects with passive or active verbs, with relational or transitive verbs, reflects a social or ideological norm for female and male behaviour. Sara Mills (1995: 45–7) provides an excellent example. She takes a short extract from Helen McInnes' novel *The Hidden Target* and analyses it for 'transitivity choices' (or who does what to whom, to put it more simply). Although finding that there does appear to be a clear patterning whereby male characters act upon women and women's body parts for more than the reverse, she does caution that:

> transitivity choices, like other linguistic choices, have a range of meanings dependent on the context in which they occur and the presuppositions which the reader brings to bear on the interpretative process.
>
> (1995: 149)

To a certain extent, while ideology appears to 'play' us, as subjects we can inflect, reject, resist or affirm the dominant heterosexual beliefs underlying such fiction. An example springs to mind: Pauline Collins, in the title role of the film 'Shirley Valentine' is wooed by her Greek holiday lover, played by Tom Conti, aboard a fishing boat. He makes an eloquent speech at one point about the intrinsic beauty of her stomach's stretch marks, where he proclaims the scars show she has lived, has survived, and they are part of her. Since she is 'lovely', they too must be 'lovely'. Turning to camera, a device used throughout to speak directly to the audience, Shirley Valentine declares that men 'talk a lot of shit'. Clearly, we cannot understand anything expressed in words just by reference to the words themselves. In reading or hearing a text, we help to select meaning. Meaning relies on all our pre-suppositions, our ability to infer and our 'world knowledge' or our understanding of how the world works. If we return to a maxim or set phrase as an example, we can understand this better:

Box 4.1 Context and meaning

'The way to a man's heart is through his stomach.'

Our ability to understand the above as a comment on heterosexual relationships and not as an extract from an anatomy manual for cardiac surgeons depends upon a range of beliefs about women's position in society. The underlying assumptions of this phrase are these:

- This is a piece of advice women want.
- Women are assumed to want to know 'the way to a man's heart'.
- Women are assumed to be heterosexual.
- Women are assumed to take on the cooking in domestic heterosexual relations.

Possibly we also have

- Men can be 'caught' by women for the small investment of culinary expertise.
- Men need to be manipulated into a relationship.
- Men are relatively easy to manipulate.
- It is presented as a transhistorical truth: it has always been, and will always be this way.
- Men base their choices of a female partner on trivial matters.

Feminists have recognised how difficult it is to attack sayings such as proverbs. The surface structure of proverbs and sayings like them is interesting to observe. As with the maxim described, they are often based on present tense verbs, especially relational verbs:

A woman's place *is* in the home.
A woman's work *is* never done.

This reflects the 'eternal truth' value of the present tense. It is like the present tense in

The earth *is* round.
The sun *sets* in the west.

The phrases are difficult, if not impossible to change. We would not conjugate the verb in any other tense, e.g.

A woman's place *will be* in the home.

Nor add a modal verb, e.g.

A woman's place *may* be in the home.

Nor yet a qualifier, e.g.

Some women's place is in the home.

Proverbs are meant to express an unerring, unchanging truth. Feminists have played with such structures to create new, feminist 'truths', altering proverbs, advertising slogans and joke punch-lines to counter inherent sexism:

A woman's place is at the bar
    in her union
    in the struggle.
A woman needs a man like a fish needs a bicycle.
The way to a man's heart is . . . oh, why bother?

Thus, words, phrases and sentences do not contain meaning in themselves. Rather, they contain elements which, when interpreted within a context (text, conversation) by a reader or listener, may lead to a range of possible readings. Some readings are more likely than others because of cultural frameworks which predispose us to read one meaning into (or out of) a phrase rather than others. These cultural frameworks are patterned by social arrangements. To take two of the previous examples:

A woman's place is in the home
The way to a man's heart is through his stomach

we can argue that both reflect certain structural arrangements in a particular society: a gender division of labour whereby women are responsible for the private, domestic arena (this holds even when women are employed in the paid workforce); inequality in relationship (women serve men's needs).

Clearly, in the case of such maxims language reflects dominant social values. However, it does not control or determine a speaker's response to them, otherwise we could not have resistance in any form. In the final chapter of this book, we will look briefly at feminist humour to develop this point further.

The vocabulary of insults and swearing

It has become something of a joke in linguistics to mention the 'thirty seven words for snow' which 'Eskimos' are meant to have. The origin of this well-rehearsed statement is now said to be a hoax. It is an example of linguistic relativity. From my position here in Dublin in the temperate zone of the Gulf Stream, I do not need thirty-seven words for snow. At a push, I have two: 'snow' and 'slush': We do have lots of words for rain and raining. A linguistic community has the words it needs to express its meanings. English has added hundreds of new words, expressions and acronyms since the 1970s to do with a range of new technologies which have emerged since then. In computing we have invented *boot up* and *toolbar* and given new meaning to *icon* and *crash*. In reproductive technology we have *GIFT, ZIFT* and notions such as *spare embryo, selective abortion, pre-implantation diagnosis* and *gene therapy*. More prosaically, we have new collocations such as *sperm bank* and *test-tube baby*. Thus, words and expressions are coined to fill lexical gaps to serve the needs of a culture or speech community.

One area of experience which is particularly interesting lexically is that of cursing, swearing and insulting people, and coinages are frequent and apparently unending. While language is said rarely if ever to produce true synonyms, it would appear that synonyms are common in the area of taboo terms. Terms develop to reflect speech community needs. An examination of the language of taboo can therefore tell us a lot about our culture's preoccupations. While Inuit people apparently have lots of words for snow, North American, British and other English speakers have lots of words for roads. We also have lots of words for women's and men's genitals and for sex acts. Many of these are used for insulting people.

Box 4.2 Positive and negative connotation

Schultz and Penelope are two feminist linguists who have drawn our attention to what Schultz has termed 'the semantic derogation of women' (Schultz [1975] in Cameron 1990 [1975]: 134). Schultz argues that it is men who have 'created English' and especially slang. Analysing the language used by men in describing women is, she claims, revealing. What appears is a catalogue of pejorated, demeaning terms reflecting men's fear, contempt or hatred of women.

Schultz traces the history of female/male word-pairs denoting the same type of person and notes that the terms relating to women became pejorated over time, as negative and sexual connotations come to be attached to them. Formerly equivalent terms become almost unrelated. Try noting, using + and −, the positive and negative connotations of the terms in the list:

bachelor	spinster, old maid
wizard	witch
lord	lady
baronet	dame
governor	governess
courtier	courtesan
master	mistress
sir	madam
king	queen

A large number of words began life meaning merely girl or woman, but today have taken on added connotations. Similarly, terms which began as complimentary have also degenerated as they have become associated only with women. Thus, *tart* now applies to a woman and is a demeaning term whereas it once referred to either sex and meant a sweet pie, just as children may be called *sugar dumpling* and the like.

Words which have not evolved to refer to women specifically, as *tart* or *wench* have done, do not undergo such pejoration. We have few terms for males which carry negative/sexual overtones. Terms which focus on sexuality tend to be positive (*rake, stud,* even *macho*). The fate of the word *macho* is revealing. It shows that it is not sufficient for feminists to coin/re-use words for the meaning to become an accepted new meaning. Words have meaning in relation to the others available and within a social context. The feminist insight which caused the word *gender* to be used alongside *sex* has been undermined by its overuse as a replacement for the word *sex*. While the feminist use aimed to draw attention to the constructed nature of our social identities, its current overuse brings us back to dichotomizing humans by biology, and gender is becoming synonymous with anatomical sex, itself claimed to be a straightforward binary opposition despite medical evidence to the contrary (Bing and Bergvall 1996: 8).

Thus the fate of feminist coinage and the semantic derogation of women reflect the same cultural bias: a sexual double standard. Men are valued for sexual prowess and women denigrated for it. But to return to the idea that vocabulary reflects a culture's needs, we can ask why there are quite so many nasty words for women (up to 2,000 in English alone). We can also ask what cultural values are reflected in the fact that our most insulting term is a slang word for female genitals and our most insulting expression invites the hearer to go away and partake in sexual intercourse, a deed many people seem to find a pleasurable rather than dreaded prospect.

Work on taboo words (Andersson and Trudgill 1992) has tended to classify swear words in three categories:

- blasphemy (*Jesus Christ! God Almighty! Bloody Hell!*)
- animal metaphor (*You cow! Pig! Bitch!*)
- 'dirty words' (*Shit! Fuck! Cunt! Bollocks!*)

Such a categorization, I believe, needs to be amended and 'nuanced' from a feminist perspective. Firstly, we should note that societal opprobrium has weakened in the case of blasphemous words. Few observe the commandment: 'Thou shalt not take the name of the Lord, thy God, in vain.' *Jesus! Christ! Oh my God!* are rarely nowadays reason for children to be censured by adults, and their milder, derivative forms (*Jeepers! Cripes! Oh my goodness!*) are hardly used. Thus, blasphemous expressions are barely even considered as swear words by many. There are no doubt a number of reasons, such as widespread secularization in Western society and the relativization of Christianity in our increasingly multicultural societies (but see Hughes 1992 for a counter position).

Animal metaphor, as a category, is amenable to feminist analysis. Most obviously, we should note that the range of available terms for insulting people is limited: we do not insult people by calling them polar bears, salmon or fruit flies. The animal terms we use refer predominantly to domesticated creatures: cow, pig, bitch, dog. Moreover, the most potent and commonly used are terms referring to female animals, usually mammals, and are used to refer to women (*cow, bitch, heifer*). Even *dog*, one of a pair (with *bitch*) and therefore most likely to refer to men as counterpart to *bitch*, now refers to a woman, especially in American English. *Pussy* also refers metonymically to woman, as well as to her genitals. (See Whaley and Antonelli 1983 for a discussion from a non-feminist standpoint).

As for the category of 'dirty' words, we should divide this into separate classifications. One sub-category are the terms related to excretion and excretory functions (*piss off, asshole, shithead* etc.)

Another is the group of terms related to heterosexual intercourse, arguably the most productive, insofar as *fuck* and its derived forms can be used to express surprise (well, fuck me!), exhaustion (I was fucked), annoyance (this fucking screwdriver), amazement, dis-appointment, anger and many other emotional states (Andersson and Trudgill 1992: 60). A further sub-set includes those which are related to women, women's bodies and specifically genitals (*cunt, twat, motherfucker*). Although taboo terms related to male genitals also exist, they do not carry the same expletive force, nor do they function in parallel. Men can be called by terms referring to female genitalia, as can women, but I have yet to hear a woman called a *prick*. Even in insult, women cannot, it seems, be honoured by epithets referring to the ultimate signifier!

The most satisfying theory to explain such use of language emerges from an attempt to see the picture whole. How do all these categories and sub-categories relate to each other? It can be argued that swear-words can be read as a code by which to decipher the very basis of **patriarchy**:

- existence of a religion based on a male god, creator of the world and creator of humans without recourse to sexual reproduction.
- a denigration of our natural, bodily functions associated with animals (hence animal metaphor, excretory swear words).
- a denigration of natural, animal reproduction.
- a denigration of women, and especially women's sexual being, hence the animal – woman connection is productive of taboo language.

A comparison with other Indo-European languages (Burgen 1996) shows similar preoccupations. I believe that the foundation of patriarchy can be 'read off' such vocabulary. It is beyond the scope of this book to spell out these connections but readers may like to follow up on these ideas by reading the works of Griffin (1978) as well as Merchant (1982), Spretnak (1982) and Adams (1996). Growing public awareness of the centrality of naming in construct-ing otherness and maintaining oppression is behind attempts to abjure offensive language. It is to this we now turn.

Politically correct language

Political correctness has been granted dictionary status: the Concise Oxford English Dictionary of 1995 defines it as 'n. the avoidance of forms of expression or action that exclude, marginalize or insult racial and cultural minorities'. The notion probably dates from the social movements and Leftist political formations of the late 1960s and the 1970s, when being 'politically correct' meant adhering to the current 'line', dogma or position of the group in question. The term now has acquired rather negative connotations and tends to be used by those who attack it, either on ideological grounds (conservatives) or tactical grounds. The most popular form of critique is ridicule, accomplished by over-zealous application of the PC principle in ludicrous coinages. Thus, detractors of PC have invented so-called PC terms such as *stolen non-human animal fibre* for *wool, incinerated non-human animal carcass* for *meat, incarcerated domestic slave* for *housewife, experientially enhanced* for *old* and *differently motivated* for *lazy.*

The issues behind the original PC movement, (race, gender, ethnicity, disability) existed before it and will survive it. Another dictionary, the American Random House Webster's College Dictionary, focuses on the more political and progressive impetus to the PC movement, defining political correctness as 'marked by or adhering to a typically progressive orthodoxy on issues involving especially race, gender, sexual affinity or ecology'. Originally, then, PC language reform aimed to make visible and give positive value to groups to which society had given secondary status, in material as well as linguistic terms. Although few really believed that changing the labels given to such groups would radically alter their social status or economic opportunities, PC language advocates did believe that more inclusive and appropriate language would have a number of other desirable effects. A good example is given by the term *African-American* or *American of African descent* to replace *Black.* An 'unpacking' of each of these terms allows us to see how word choice might affect thought processes. If we call a person *Black* or *White,* we are defining the person by skin-colour, as if skin-colour in itself summarized the salient characteristics of that person. If, on the other hand, we use the term *American of African descent,* we focus on the person's political status (citizenship) and her or his history. We name, however indirectly, the experience of slavery. In many contexts, neither skin colour nor ancestry are strictly relevant to the social requirements of a speech event. However, while ancestry constitutes a historical and cultural feature affecting social being in an acutely personal way, skin colour only has salience in a racist society. Skin colour *in itself* has no meaning, just as biological sex *in itself* has no meaning. It is racist and sexist societies which determine what meaning will be given to being white or black, to being female or male, which social slots people fit into, which educational opportunities will be available and so on. The same is true of class divisions and of religious and ethnic divisions in sectarian societies.

As well as re-naming oppressed groups, the PC movement succeeded, in the USA especially, in re-evaluating the experience of the groups so renamed. University courses had for decades focused on the literature, history and science of a privileged group, dubbed DWEMs (Dead White European Males). The corpus of work of such men had been the unquestioned 'canon'. Political and social movement activists began to challenge this hegemonic position and the works of marginalized groups began to feature in such courses. Women's Studies courses, Black literature courses, Lesbian and Gay or, more recently Queer Studies began to be developed. Such has been the challenge to the white-male-as-norm underpinning of university education that Men's Studies are now being developed. Although many feminists argue that 'Men's Studies' don't need to be taught because almost all study has focused on men up to now, the launching of such courses has the merit of recognizing that men's experience is not general or generalizable to women, that it is specific. An implicit challenge to the male-as-norm, male as reference point philosophy is made. Detractors of the PC challenge to the canon do, of course, argue that the reason DWEM works have been honoured and become the canon is that they are the best.

We may note a certain similarity in the ridicule feminist language reform and PC language reform have encountered. There is also a similarity in the underlying aims of such language reform. Fifteen years before PC became a cultural buzzword, feminists had begun to argue that to change women's social being, we needed to change the language which reflected our secondary status. This was no more true than in the language used in job advertisements. This area provides a good example of how changing the language does alter perception, and even behaviour.

Names of professions and occupations

Names for professions and occupations often cause a gender-stereotyped mental image to be conjured up. Consider the following riddle:

> A man and his son were involved in a serious road accident, the
> father being killed outright. The boy, with serious head injuries,
> was taken by ambulance to the nearest hospital and prepared for
> brain surgery. The neuro-surgeon entered the O.T., looked at the
> child and exclaimed: I can't operate on him. This is my son.
> How can this be?

The majority of people are unable to answer this riddle. The surgeon is the boy's mother. When we hear 'brain-surgeon' or 'neuro-
surgeon', we have a mental image corresponding to the name: a
man in a white/green coat, a mask and latex gloves. Similarly, masculine images are conjured up by words like 'engineer', 'nuclear
physicist' and 'architect', although theoretically such words are epicenes, that is, they can apply to women or men. As we saw earlier,
pronoun use reinforces the masculine imagery associated with the
words, and a gender division of labour limiting women's participation at the upper end of the job market makes the masculine imagery seem appropriate.

If epicene terms make us think only of males, then terms with
the suffix -*man* are even more likely to do so. How many women
are likely to apply for jobs when advertisements proclaim the
employer is looking for a *draughtsman, repairman* or *salesman?*
This is one area where feminist agitation in the early 1970s led to
formal changes. Employment equality legislation, enacted throughout the member states of what was then the EEC (now EU) made
discrimination on the basis of sex illegal, and various countries set
up commissions to invent or adjust the vocabulary for designating
specific occupations and professions. The ways to do this depend
upon the particular language. In languages with grammatical gender, such as French or German, the preferred option has been
feminization of terms which previously had only masculine forms.
In German, this involves in most cases the simple addition of the
suffix '-in' to the job titles. Thus, we have *Artz* (doctor(m)) and
Ärtzin (doctor (f)), *Präsidentin* (president (f)) and *Präsident* (president
(m)). Another option has been to use *Frau* (woman) as a suffix,
by dropping the capital F (all nouns in German use initial capitals).
Thus, the female equivalent of *Artz* may now be *Artzfrau* rather
than *Ärtzin* and a number of such neologisms have been formed:
Medienfrau, Armeefrau, Filmfrau and *Architekturfrau,* for example. The
problem arises in the plural. If we wish to talk about doctors, archi-
tects, which term should we use in German or other grammatical
gender languages? In the past, the masculine plural was used and
was supposed to include female and male incumbents. This is

still the case in French. German has invented a new spelling for plurals to draw attention to the deliberate inclusion of the feminine by using a capital letter in the middle of the word:

Gesucht: VolljuristInnen
Vacancy for female / male qualifier lawyer.

The other option is to split plurals to mention both females and males separately:

Leserinnen und Leser (female and male readers).

In French, progress has been more difficult, at least in France itself. In French-speaking Canada (Quebec), progress in this area has been faster and more radical reforms have been achieved. This proves that arguments about the language itself resisting such neologisms are invalid. Where there is a (social) will, there is a way. Swiss, Belgian and Quebec French have changed more rapidly than French in France and it is social, political and cultural factors which determine change.

An interesting point to note regarding French in France, is that there has never been a shortage of specifically feminine forms for all those jobs at the lower end of the social and pay scales: *ménagère, serveuse, servante, femme de ménage, assistante, aide-soignante, institutrice, infirmière*. It is only at the top end that the rare women who attain such prestigious positions have to make do with masculine forms: *Madame le maire* (mayor), *Madame le ministre* (minister) *Madame le conseiller régional* (regional assembly councillor) and so on. Some argue that the women themselves prefer the masculine term, as it draws attention to the scarcity of women in their position, thus reinforcing their success. A more likely argument is that the feminine form of many occupational titles referring to high-status professions referred in the past and still refers today to the wife of a man in the position. Thus *Monsieur le pharmacien* (the pharmacist), *Madame la pharmacienne* (the pharmacist's wife). This usage is destined to die out as women are referred to by their own achievements, rather than those of a husband. This will free up all those feminine forms to be used for the growing number of women in the professions.

In English, the opposite process has been preferred. Words like *poetess, actress, sculptress, manageress* and expressions like *lady-doctor* have been replaced by the epicene forms *poet, actor, sculptor, manager* and *doctor*. The problem then arises with pronouns when such words are used generically. What do we put in the gap in sentences like the following?

- A good doctor is one who will always do a house call when ___ is needed.
- If an architect had done that to my house I'd bring ___ to court.

Mental imagery may still favour men even if women are using forms like *actor* and *manager* to refer to themselves. If we change *fireman* to *fire-fighter*, are we still more likely to picture a man? Some French feminists argue that the neutralization of masculine forms into epicenes actually does a disservice to women, making women even less visible socially and professionally. However, it seems inappropriate for feminists in one linguistic community to comment on the strategies used in other linguistic communities. The -*ess* suffix or *lady* prefix in English has traditionally connoted amateurism or dilettantism. This has been unfair and discriminatory. If we were to extend the use of such suffixes or prefixes as the French and Germans have done, the result would be that terms like *doctor, writer* and *architect* would denote only men. In the plural then, we would need to write *doctors* and *doctresses, writers* and *writresses* (if we take *waiter* and *waitress* as our model) or *doctors* and *lady-doctors, dentists* and *lady-dentists*. Clearly this is unacceptable. There is not one way for all languages to be reformed for greater gender inclusiveness. Indeed, there may be several solutions within one and the same language. French itself does use epicenes: *le* or *la journaliste, le* or *la chimiste* for example.

Changing the language is not enough. Changing social structures, educational and professional opportunities is also necessary. Language will (eventually) follow. Some consider such language change as trivial and argue that feminists should focus on more important things like equal pay, confronting the glass ceiling, free child care. These aims are not mutually exclusive. Research does show that inclusive language in job advertisements does mean more women apply for the position. And sometimes they even get them!

Summary

- the vocabulary of a language reflects a speech community's needs

- women and men are named very differently in the English language

- terms referring to women undergo pejoration

- taboo terms reflect the hatred or fear of women

- language reform does not always work as expected and social change is more likely to lead to change in language than the reverse

Further reading

Bodine, Ann 1975 'Androcentrism in prescriptive grammar: singular *they*, sex-indefinite *he*, and *he or she*', in *Language in Society* 4, reprinted in Cameron, D. (ed.) 1990 *The feminist critique of language: a reader*, Routledge, London and New York, pp. 166–86.

Cameron, Deborah 1995 *Verbal hygiene*, Routledge, London and New York.

Mills, Sara 1995 *Feminist stylistics*, Routledge, London and New York, Chapter 5: 'Analysis at the level of the phrase/sentence', pp. 128–58.

Schultz, Muriel R. 1975 'The semantic derogation of women', in Thorne Barrie and Henley Nancy (eds) *Language and sex: difference and dominance*, Newbury House, Rowley, MA., reprinted in Cameron, Deborah (ed.) *The feminist critique of language: a reader*, Routledge, London and New York, pp. 134–47.

Spender, Dale 1985 *Man-made language* (2nd edition) Routledge and Kegan Paul, London and New York, Chapter 6: 'The politics of naming', pp. 163–90.

PART TWO

Chapter 5

Language in use:
feminist perspectives

Chapter outline

In Part I, we looked at language as a system and explored the question of the sexist nature (or otherwise) of the English language. The focus in Part I was on what the language can, does, does not, cannot say and cannot avoid saying about women and men and about social and cultural realities.

In Part II, we will be looking at how speakers actually use language when interacting with others. Do women and men differ in their use of language? If so, in what ways? Some researchers, feminist and malestream, have argued that there are differences; others, especially feminists, have argued that much of the research has been flawed, the findings inconclusive, and the interpretations biased. Yet others have argued that there are more similarities than differences, or that we are not asking the right questions. A vast literature now exists on the topic of women and men in interaction. This chapter will introduce the area by examining the following topics:

- methods in sociolinguistics and treatment of gender
- feminist critiques of sociolinguistics
- gender in feminist theory
- difference and dominance approaches
- critique of sex-difference research framework and methodologies

Contextualizing feminist sociolinguistics

A great deal of linguistics has, traditionally, been carried out without reference to actual speakers in real-life circumstances. The search for a comprehensive set of rules to describe the English language, for example, has been carried out by linguists using introspection and native-speaker intuition as a method to access 'real language'. In general, the real language of Anglophone linguists has been standard or prestige educated British or American English, that is to say, their own.

Early sociolinguistics, in the form of dialectology, broke with introspection, and sought out speakers of non-standard varieties. Fieldworkers travelled to relatively remote areas to record the lexical variation and pronunciation of vocabulary items related largely to agriculture and rural domestic life. The result was a series of linguistic atlases. Many such studies were based by choice on elderly male informants in rural areas. Researchers often felt that such men were the best informants because it was thought that they preserved the dialect in its purest form; cut off from social intercourse by the nature of agricultural work, they were seen by many researchers to be least likely to come under the influence of standard or other dialects. This view was not unanimous, however, and other researchers favoured female informants. Women, confined to the domestic environment, were least likely to contaminate their speech with words from elsewhere, it was argued. A minority of studies required fieldworkers to interview both women and men (Coates 1993: 47–57).

The development and increased visibility since the late 1960s of a variety of emancipatory social movements in Western countries and elsewhere have drawn attention to the notion of group specificity (Gibbon 1993). Lesbians, bisexuals and gays came out of the closet and proclaimed the right to be treated equally with straights, while refusing to be the same. The Northern Ireland civil rights activists publicly demonstrated for equal rights for Catholics; in the USA, Black civil rights activists did likewise; students and young people in general developed a youth counter-culture and women also began to identify as different. Trade unionism underwent a period of radicalization in a number of countries. Regional minorities formed advocate groups to fight for economic and political equality as well as cultural and linguistic rights. Women revived the feminist movement which had suffered a severe attack since the immediate post-war period, and had gone into relative decline. Such social ferment did not go unnoticed in the universities; indeed, many academics were, themselves, at the forefront of these social movements.

Sociolinguistics was directly affected by the new visibility of groups proclaiming their difference from the relatively unchallenged white, male, heterosexual, middle-class norm. It became clear that all these different groups in society would have their own linguistic identities too. Sociolinguists set out to study them. To the traditional variables of class and of geographic origin were added those of 'race' and ethnic group, age and – of specific interest to us here – gender. Or rather sex, since at that stage the feminist theorization of gender was just beginning (again).

In former times, universities had been happy to view disciplines as equally important and many of the world's best-known thinkers combined the study of science, religion, mathematics and the arts. By the 1960s, however, disciplines were organized in a hierarchy with science at the top and arts at the bottom. A number of arts subjects, linguistics among them, re-christened themselves as social 'sciences' to increase their status and funding. This had an effect on method, since 'hard' scientific methods were adopted and adapted for use in these disciplines. Early sociolinguistic studies used quantitative methods to show how linguistic features correlated with social structures. While these are still the methods used today, these instruments have been refined and a number of problems, especially that of bias in interpretation, have been eliminated or reduced, partly as a result of feminist critique.

Positivist sociolinguistics is then based on the idea that researchers can observe, quantify, describe and interpret linguistic variables and show how these vary according to the speaker's class, age, gender and so on. Obviously, in linguistics, it is important to have reliable data, and this from the outset posed a number of problems. Good data are not easy to come by. There are problems of a technical nature, such as the quality of recordings, but the effects of the tape-recorder and of being observed or studied pose even greater problems. If speakers know the researcher wants to find out whether they say 'drinking' or 'drinkin', they will actively monitor their own speech and the researcher will not get the naturally occurring speech they would hear in a non-experimental setting. This problem is call the 'observer's paradox'.

To circumvent this problem, researchers use a variety of methods. One such method is tacit recording. Subjects are not told they are being recorded. Some feminists object to this on ethical grounds, as they do to studies where subjects are led to believe that the study is about something else, and hence may not monitor their speech. Another method, devised by William Labov and adopted by others, is to ask for emotionally charged information in the hope that the recounting of say, a life-threatening experience, will override the speaker's linguistic control mechanisms and cause them to speak naturally during the research interview. Another method used to obtain vernacular speech is to have fieldwork done by helpers who are similar to, or members of, the group being studied. Presumably, speakers would not monitor and alter their speech patterns in the presence of a researcher who looks and sounds like a member of the peer group. Thus, white researchers employed young black male fieldworkers to collect data on Black English vernacular (BEV), the English spoken by young black urban males. This precaution is not always taken by researchers, with the result that subjects (informants) do consciously or unconsciously alter their normal speech habits. They may try to speak more like the fieldworker/researcher, more like the standard or they may exaggerate their speech to conform to the norms of their peer group in order to mark their difference from the interviewer. We know intuitively that some people do alter their speech patterns in this way: we may know someone who has a 'telephone voice'. Try listening carefully to the recorded messages on phone-answering machines of your friends and relatives; you will probably find some degree of shift or accommodation towards the standard, and a relative downplaying of regional pronunciation features.

As well as knowing intuitively that people shift in this way, we know it from research carried out in the early 1970s by sociolinguist Peter Trudgill on the English spoken in his native Norwich. After recording the pronunciation of a range of linguistic variables such as the vowel sound in words like *gate, face, tame* and in *ear, here, idea,* variables such as the 'in' or 'ing' pronunciation at the end of words like *eating, walking,* Trudgill invited his informants to report on their own usage of such pronunciations (Trudgill 1972). He played the informants tape recordings of words spoken with the non-standard and standard pronunciations and asked which was the pronunciation they personally produced. Although a number of speakers reported accurately on their pronunciation, many did not. Some over-reported their use of non-standard forms and some under-reported their use of non-standard forms. Despite some degree of overlap between female and male speakers, women tended to over-report use of the standard and men to under-report use of the standard.

The fact that speakers can attempt an answer to such a question, and the fact that they can be mistaken about their own usage, shows that they are aware that different pronunciations are socially 'loaded'. Trudgill explained women's greater use of standard forms and aspiration to standard forms by reference to their sensitivity to non-material matters of social status. Denied opportunities to establish social status by employment, he argued, women focus on appearance to project it. He explained men's tendency to under-report use of the standard by the covert prestige of the non-standard form, which Trudgill claimed carries a connotation of toughness or masculinity.

A number of criticisms can be, and have been, made of both Trudgill's and Labov's research by feminists (James 1996). While Labov was criticized for studying only male speakers of BEV, in his 1972 studies, Trudgill was criticized for bias in interpreting his data. Trudgill was not alone in the early 1970s in using an inadequate class-structure model to stratify his informants. Christine Delphy has shown the problems inherent in classifying women according to the social class of their fathers or husbands (1984). She argues that social-stratification studies fail to account for women's class position and actually obscure their status as dependants. If women are classified by their husband's profession then a woman who is married to a judge and is a housewife shares the same class position as a woman who is herself a judge and married to another professional. In claiming that women (as a group) seek overt prestige linguistically while men (as a group) seek covert prestige, Trudgill actually misrepresents his own findings. If the standard or prestige variables are associated with middle-class norms and non-standard with working-class norms, then middle-class women's and working-class men's linguistic behaviour is in line with expectations. We only need then to account for working-class or lower-middle-class women's adoption of middle-class norms, and middle-class or lower-middle-class men's adoption of working-class norms, as these run counter to expectation. The explanation could lie in a reinterpretation of the standard in terms of a norm of middle-class usage and/or of female usage. The working-class speech patterns may connote something other than toughness or masculinity to women. They may carry sexual connotations too (Gordon:1994). Moreover, Trudgill implicitly took working-class men's speech to represent working-class speech, thus presenting it as a norm against which to measure working-class women's speech. This was then seen as deviating from this norm. If the social class stratification model inaccurately placed women in this class (e.g. female clerical worker married to factory hand) then women's linguistic behaviour which was in line with their own occupational status would be judged to be anomalous when judged according to the class position attributed to them on the basis of their husband's occupation. (James in Bergvall *et al.* 1996: 106). Ultimately, what we find in Trudgill's study is the all too common tendency to explain gender difference in terms of class or class in terms of gender. It points up the need to recognize that there is not a unified experience of being working class: it is inflected by gender and other variables like ethnic group. No doubt there is also no unified experience of being a woman: it too is inflected by class and other variables. Unfortunately a huge amount of research proceeds as if women formed one big homogeneous group and men another, including a large body of feminist research. The criticisms some feminists have levelled against mainstream researchers like Trudgill can equally be levelled at some of the work done by feminists, especially work in the 1970s.

How we understand sex, or gender, lies at the heart of all research on women's and men's language. In order to understand the debates – sometimes heated – between different feminist positions, we need to understand the different ways that women and men can be conceptualized. What is a woman? What is a man? Are there differences? What are they? Where do they come from? Could they be different? Are there similarities? Why do we rarely ask that question? Is gender given at birth? Is it the same as sex? Is it something we have, like blue eyes? Or is it something we do, like shave our legs or dye our hair? It is questions like these and the answers given to them which divide feminists into a variety of camps with more or less moving boundaries. Crucially, it is questions like these and researchers' answers to them which underlie the design of studies and the interpretation of results.

There is not one movement called 'feminism'; indeed an influential book on the women's movement in France pluralized the word in its title: *New French feminisms: an anthology* (1981). The editors, Marks and De Courtivron, recognized implicitly the doctrinal differences which existed between various strands within the French movement. The need to write books about French feminism for English speakers also pointed up the fact that feminism is inflected in each country by local conditions and by national intellectual traditions. British feminism has enjoyed a stronger relationship with left-wing politics than French feminism, which, in one of its forms, has been affected by the neo-Freudian psychoanalytic movement. American feminism has, at least outside the universities, been influenced by that country's strong individualism so that liberal feminism has developed strongly there, especially among white women. Women whose experience of gender oppression is coupled with oppression on the grounds of ethnic or racial discrimination have developed theory and practice to understand and combat their specific experiences of oppression. Feminism is often related to national liberation movements in anti-imperialist struggles. Some lesbian feminists, though not all, fight alongside gay men against homophobia or heterosexism. It is not always easy to combine feminism with other struggles carried out in mixed groups. The attempt of socialist-feminism or Marxist-feminism in the 1970s and 1980s to combine class politics with feminism was particularly fraught. One participant quipped that a socialist-feminist was one who 'went to twice as many meetings'.

How can we make sense of all these different groups and how does this relate to language and gender? The simplest way to make sense of the groups is to ask how they understand or conceptualize the gender division in our societies. The relevance for language and gender research is that in linguistics too, feminists are divided along similar lines to feminists in general. It is beyond the scope of an introductory work to examine these doctrinal differences in detail. In drawing up the following rough guide which aims to flesh out the brief introduction given in Chapter 1, I am aware that I am imposing boundaries upon a relatively fluid reality.

We can begin with what feminists have in common. Feminists oppose the unequal treatment of women and men and the belief system which upholds it. Under this belief system (variously called reductionism, naturalism or patriarchal thought), differences between women and men are said to be of natural or biological origin. The exact aspect of our biology which is said to cause all the social distinctions made between the sexes has changed at different periods: body size and weight, fat-to-muscle ratio, blood temperature, hormonal profile, our reproductive systems and structure of the brain have all been invoked to 'explain' the system which makes sex salient for dividing human beings into two very differently treated groups in society. Belief in a biological basis for social inequality is at the heart of patriarchal thought. Reducing social inequality to a biological cause is a type of thinking which is least likely to admit of change and protest. In other words, if the inequalities between women and men are innate, given in nature, derive from our biology, then there would be no point trying to change anything (Delphy 1984).

One of twentieth-century feminism's earliest, most profound and enduring contributions to our understanding of women's inferior status in the world was the theorization of the concept of gender. Making the distinction between sex, seen as natural and pre-given (but see Bing and Bergvall 1996: 8), and gender, seen as social, cultural and constructed, was a turning point for feminism. The theorization of gender construction is at the heart of the impressive and elaborate feminist literature of our time. Feminism's understanding that differences between women and men derived not from some supposedly innate characteristics but from the way we are positioned relative to each other in society, was taken up by the social and natural sciences and led to an explosion of research in anthropology, sociology, politics, biology and linguistics to name a few.

We noted in Chapter 4 that the term 'gender' is gradually replacing 'sex' in a wide variety of text types and in speech. This could stem from a general misunderstanding of the difference intended by feminists in marking the two as distinct, from a reluctance to accept the feminist insight that gender does not automatically map on to or equate with sex, or from a desire to silence feminist opposition to patriarchal ways of knowing, to patriarchal truth. We noted how the feminist coinage *Ms*, invented to replace *Miss* and *Mrs*, has in practice, come to be added to them on official forms. For some, *Ms* means 'divorced' or 'separated'. The desire to mark women's status relative to men (as unmarried, married, divorced) only makes sense in a patriarchal society where women are not accorded independent status on a par with men and need to have their sexual un/availability signalled.

Box 5.1 Gender identities

Let us indulge for a moment in a little science/politics fiction in order to grasp the full import of the feminist distinction between sex and gender. Imagine a world in which, upon birth, instead of proclaiming 'it's a boy!' or 'it's a girl!', midwives and obstetricians announced 'it's a brown!' or 'it's a blue!', after looking into the eyes of the baby. The presence of a vulva, clitoris and vagina or testicles and penis would, in this society, be irrelevant. This is a society where eye colour is used as a marker to divide all persons into two groups. Just as nowadays intersexed infants are 'corrected' to fit into one of the only two sexes recognized (Bing and Bergvall 1996: 10), children with grey or green eyes would be fitted as soon as possible with blue or brown contact lenses or undergo gene therapy to alter their eye colour to become an acceptable blue or brown. Continuing our analogy, let us imagine that the friends and relatives now go off to buy presents and send cards to the happy parents of the new blue or brown. The stationer's shop offers cards with a blue background, welcoming the new blue, and with a brown background, welcoming the new brown. They note the different wording on the cards. Apparently parents must feel delighted with their beautiful brown who'll give them so much joy and pleasure and are so thrilled to have a blue who will make them proud, be fun and adventurous and get into all kinds of mischief. Next stop is the baby shop: pretty, pastel, fluffy toys for browns and lots of frilly clothes too; for blues, brightly coloured stimulating activity centres and practical denim dungarees for hard wear during all that mischievous exploring.

Blues and browns will be segregated at playschool. Browns will enjoy playing quietly and blues will go off exploring. Browns will pay attention to the brown teacher and blues will be disruptive and seek all the attention, by being naughty if necessary. The brown teacher will give blues more attention and excuse their behaviour because everyone knows blue-eyed children are naturally more active, independent and have more energy than browns, tend to interrupt and compete with other children and sometimes use bad language. Blues particularly dislike browns and when they fall out with a blue friend will even insult them. If the friend gets upset, the blue will accuse the friend of being 'just like a brown!' Browns easily get hurt feelings because they are sensitive and need to relate to people.

You get the point. Feminists argued from the 1970s that our gender identities are constructed. Simone de Beauvoir had said, famously, 'On ne naît pas femme, on le devient' (one is not *born* a woman, it is something one *becomes*). We learn how to be acceptable women (and men), and our parents, teachers and peers constantly remind us of how to behave. If it really was 'natural' to be a woman or a man, why do people spend so much time telling children how to do it? 'Big boys don't cry.' 'It's not ladylike to sit like that.' 'Girls shouldn't swear.'

The fact that gender prescriptions are arbitrary is proved by anthropologists who note that what is considered masculine in one culture, would be appropriate for women in another. Ann Oakley in *Sex, gender and society* (1972: 58) quotes anthropologist William

Davenport who describes adornment among the people of a South-west Pacific community he studied:

> Only men wear flowers in their hair and scented leaves tucked into their belts or arm bands. At formal dances it is the man who dresses in the most elegant finery and . . . when these young men are fully made up and costumed for the dance they are considered so irresistible to women that they are not allowed to be alone, even for a moment, for fear some women will seduce them.

Moreover, anthropology has also described societies where more than the two genders of the West are accepted and named (Hall and O'Donovan 1996: 228). Although in the West, we only offi-cially recognize two sexes, female and male, and 'cure' intersexed infants by surgery or hormonal treatments, nonetheless, as we saw in Chapter 1, we do have a vocabulary to describe a wide range of gender positions and sexual orientations/choices. The existence of this vocabulary proves the inadequacy of our two-way split into women and men and our long-time unquestioned assumption of a heterosexual norm. The naming of heterosexuality itself witnesses its demise as an unquestioned norm.

Gender then has become the cornerstone of feminist analysis, but, in practice, feminists do not agree on what we should do with it. Knowing that our behaviour, social roles and positions and the value society places on women are learned and arbitrary led to a variety of responses.

In an early analysis of the French women's movement, split like others into opposing factions, sociologist Garcia-Guadilla (1981) argued that, in the post-war Western world, two diametrically opposed global tendencies were being played out. On the one hand, we can witness homogenizing tendency where countries, markets, cultural products like TV programmes, consumer goods, tastes and lifestyles are becoming more and more similar (globalization). We think of the significance of Coca-Cola™ whose logo is recognized world-wide or of the Nike™ swoosh coveted by teenagers in many countries. We think of the loss of traditional ways of life and ethnic specificity as remote populations are drawn into the world market economy, and the concomitant loss of lesser-spoken languages. Here in Dublin as I write, an indigenous pharmacy chain has recently been bought by Boots, the British chain, an Irish supermarket chain bought by Tesco's, and British clothing stores now populate all the large Irish shopping malls. A recent *Time* magazine article by James Geary (7 July 1997) calculated that half the world's 6,500 or so languages were in danger of extinction due to such homo-genizing tendencies. One approach to gender is towards a similar homogenizing tendency, with 'globalization' occurring in the dir-ection of the spread of masculine values, behaviour and styles. Women are the ones, like the minority ethnic groups, who accom-modate to male-defined behaviour. Liberal feminism works in this direction. Recognizing that the gender roles of women led to non-paid or under-paid positions, liberal feminists and their organiza-tions promoted sameness or homogeneity using masculine style as a model. Women competed within the system with men, seeking equality of opportunity, education, training, pay and promotion in the workplace. In the 1980s this was reflected in fashion with power dressing, sharp suits and by shoulder pads for women, and in assertiveness training.

The second and opposing tendency Garcia-Guadilla outlined was a heterogenizing tendency, where instead of embracing same-ness social groups espouse and celebrate difference. We think of the social movements referred to earlier. Breton parents send their children to Diwan (the seed) schools to be educated through Breton rather than French while Irish parents set up Gaelscoileanna (Irish medium schools). Instead of turning to the East for spir-itual enlightenment, Westerners explore lost native traditions such as Celtic shamanism or Druidry. Instead of dancing to the sound of rock and roll, all over the world, traditional ethnic music is being revived (and marketed) for young people to dance to. Witness the 'world music' section in large music stores. Within feminism, a strong current emerged in the 1980s which, far from embracing masculine values and joining in masculine pursuits, actively celeb-rated what it viewed as women's difference, women's values and women's culture.

Let us use an analogy to examine these two opposing strategies. Imagine a group of ethnically different immigrants in a new coun-try. Perhaps the group is visibly different from the 'host' commun-ity, wears traditional dress, eats ethnic food, calls its children by ethnic names and speaks its own language. Such a group, faced with numerical and political superiority of the native population, can choose to remain separate and different by living and work-ing as far as possible in areas of similar people, continuing to speak their own language and rear their children through the language, inculcating their values and religious beliefs to them and avoiding contact with the host culture (ghettoization). Alternately they can live dispersed throughout the new community, adopt the majority language, clothing, eating habits and religion, give their children host culture names, perhaps even alter their own surnames and in every possible way pass as a native of the new country (assimilation). Another option is to become bilingual, to maintain cultural specificity but to take up a third place (Kramsch 1993) adopting an intercultural perspective. It would, of course, be naïve to imagine that the host nation welcomes any or all of these strategies. Assimilation depends on acceptance by the host and carries a cost of loss of authenticity. Remaining unintegrated means feeling like a stranger in a foreign land and risking endless misunderstanding when contact *is* necessary, as it inevitably is. The attempts to take up a 'third place' as cultural mediators can easily be misconstrued by one's peers and the native population alike. The taking up of a 'third place' may only be possible between groups viewed at the outset as equals.

Feminists and women in general have been faced with this kind of dilemma before the gender divide, and the rich and contradictory feminist literature reflects the variety of positions women can take. While liberal feminists have fought for formal equality with men in the workplace, socialist feminists have pointed out that this changes the women (who succeed) but not the world. Men are not equal amongst themselves, they argue, so how can women seek equality with 'men'. Which men? Essentially, they are adding a critique of capitalist class relations to their concern for women's liberation from domination by men. Another group of feminists, considered radical by virtue of their prioritizing patriarchy, not capitalism, as the root of women's oppression, argue that socialist feminists fail to recognize the benefits even working-class men derive from the gender system. All three of these sub-groups agree that men, as a gender, benefit from the current arrangement and that women can and should wrest this privilege from men. This is an enormously simplified and schematic account given simply to put into context what has been called the *dominance approach* in feminist critiques of language.

This approach is often contrasted with the *difference approach*, common to American cultural feminism and French psychoanalytic feminism which (largely misunderstood) partly inspired the American current. The most popular texts, known to the general public, fall within this approach (Gray 1993, Tannen 1990). Instead of recognizing men's greater privilege, access to power and resources as something to be wrested from men, women in these groups have argued for a re-evaluation of the feminine side of the gender division. This has involved an embracing of women's specificity. Whether learned or innate (not all cultural feminists agree on this), women's ways, values, style and culture are valuable, even preferable to men's. Why emulate masculine values which promote competition, destruction, war and ecological destruction, they ask. Some feminists have claimed that women's traditional roles as carers and nurturers have made them morally superior to men (Gilligan 1982, Daly 1978); others appear at times to claim that women are innately superior, as if women carried some kind of gene for relating, for ecological responsibility or for caring and nurturing (Griffin 1978, Raymond 1986).

To materialist feminist writers and theorists (Delphy 1984, Guillaumin in Duchen 1987, Segal 1987 and Hartmann 1981) difference is inequality and to claim one's difference as a woman is a feminist own goal. It is tantamount, Delphy argues, to claiming the right to be oppressed, marginalized and exploited. To French feminists of the Psychanalyse et Politique group, however, *not* to claim one's difference is to collude in the most extreme form of oppression, that of the non-recognition of women as women. If women fight to share men's power and privilege, they argue, then all we are seeing is women copying men, women giving value to male culture and male hierarchy, male power structures and male knowledge. Women they say, have to rid themselves of the phallus in their heads. This, they argue, can only be done if women develop a woman's way of being, of thinking, of speaking. To do so, women need to re-invent language. Men's language, they claim, cannot express women's consciousness, women's authentic voice, women's bodily experience. Feminists within this tendency and sympathetic to it, have been at the forefront of a literary movement involving experimental writing, and their influence has spread, by translation, to feminists in North American, including Canadian, universities. This cultural transfer is, itself, the subject of feminist theory (Simon 1996, von Flotow 1997).

The re-evaluation of women's strengths, styles or culture came to be applied within feminist linguistics. Since Jespersen (1922 [1964]) and later Lakoff (1975) described the language use of women and men as different (with women's patterns seen as deficient viewed against a male norm), some feminist linguists began to re-evaluate those patterns identified as typical of women and to stress the positive aspects of their conversational or interactional styles. An enormous number of studies were carried out, largely in response to Lakoff's 1975 publication, on just about every linguistic feature imaginable, from use of questions, intonation patterns, swearing and slang, adverbs, interruptions, sentence length and feedback. The next chapter reviews this research in detail.

The existence of two models – the difference model and the dominance model – mean that research findings can be interpreted in two different ways. If we find a difference between women and men on some variable such as tendency to interrupt, we can interpret this in a way which reinforces gender difference (it is just that women and men have different styles) or in a way that challenges gender (difference is inequality and men dominate women socially and linguistically).

The next section examines critically the sex-difference approach by confronting its premises with those of the dominance approach. However, we need to go beyond this division into two schools for a number of reasons, not least the fact that such a division is schematic and that good research has been done on both sides of the divide. Another important reason is that there is now a competing framework for examining gender which goes beyond both of these approaches, the postmodernist.

Sex-difference research: a critique

It is impossible to begin to analyse the difference approach without referring to Robin Lakoff's 1975 work, *Language and woman's place*. It has been influential in two ways: firstly, it has inspired a huge amount of empirical work carried out to test its assertions about women's style; secondly, it has inspired a vast critical literature and led to the development of a variety of counter-positions.

Lakoff wrote her monograph from within mainstream linguistics. Unlike emerging sociolinguistics work which was empirically based and focused on the vernacular, Lakoff used the traditional method of introspection and native-speaker intuition to describe what she called 'women's language'. Women, she claimed, used language differently from men. She proceeded to describe what she viewed as typical or characteristic features and to give examples. Basically she argued that women's speech forms expressed uncertainty, deference, politeness, insecurity and emotionality. The picture she painted was of rather deficient users of language in general. Women were said, for example, to use empty adjectives like 'adorable' and 'divine', to avoid the swear words men typically used, replacing them with attenuated expletives like 'goodness' or 'oh dear', and to end statements with tag questions to mitigate the strength of their opinions or observations. She claimed that women, instead of saying something like

'The situation in the Lebanon is awful'

would prefer a form like

'The situation in the Lebanon is awful, isn't it?'

or

'The situation in the Lebanon is awful, don't you think?'

This assertion was based on Lakoff's intuition or her impressions of friends' speech habits, as pointed out earlier.

Apart from arguing that empirical studies are the only way to check if women and men do not use this feature with roughly similar frequency, critics of Lakoff also argued that tag questions perform more than one function. In other words, her interpretation of the use of tags to mean hesitancy or lack of confidence in asserting an opinion needs to be nuanced. Tags, as questions, function to invite a comment by the other speaker/s in an interaction. Instead of being a sign of a deficient speaker, a tag question can be a sign of a competent conversationalist who knows how to include others. Coates, especially in her recent *Women talk* (1996) and West in her recent article 'Women's competence in conversation' (1995) take issue with the 'deficiency' interpretation of features such as tags and argue that they are multifunctional. Between women friends at least, tag questions do not always lead to a switch in speaker, and often receive only supportive minimal responses which allow the speaker to continue. Some tags are used to seek information:

Helen: You haven't been applying for jobs as well *have you?*

(Coates 1996: 192)

In the next chapter we will look in detail at research findings on these topics.

I want to conclude this chapter with a general critique which focuses on conceptualization and methodology in sex-difference research and upon the implications for women in general of the research findings which are published and disseminated to a wider public.

Feminists who had begun to conceptualize the construction of gender in the early 1970s were heartened by a ground-breaking book by two social psychologists, Maccoby and Jacklin's *The psychology of sex differences* (1974). The authors had analyzed and summarized over 2,000 experimental studies (this type of work is called a meta-analysis) and concluded that commonly held beliefs about gender differences were generally far off the mark. Their study showed that many deeply held beliefs about women's and men's behaviour, aptitudes, strengths and weaknesses were exaggerated and largely based on prejudice. The study showed that similarities and overlaps tended to be ignored, especially in reports on such studies published for the general public. Difference, it seemed, was publishable and desired, similarity was not.

Similar meta-analyses have been carried out since, particularly in the field of social psychology but also within sociolinguistics (James and Drakich 1993, James and Clarke 1993). What such large-scale studies show is that results are often contradictory, but the success of best-sellers like Tannen's *You just don't understand* (1990) or Gray's *Men are from Mars, women are from Venus* (1993) suggests that the actual complexity of results and their contradictory nature are unwelcome. We live in a male-dominated society in which men control more resources, are better paid, own far more property, have more status and are granted more autonomy than women. In order for this to continue, for social structures to be maintained, belief in and reproduction of gender is crucial. Gender difference is a central organizing principle of our society and huge efforts are made to ensure its continuation. This fact is no less true in universities or publishing houses. It has been conclusively shown that studies showing little or no variation between women and men will receive much less publicity than those which do. Small differences will be exaggerated or misinterpreted (Aries 1997: 91), especially if we focus on statistically significant differences rather than effect sizes (how big a difference we mean). Factors which may have an effect during experiments like relative age, social class, status or role, and task or function are often ignored, so that it is not clear that sex (or gender) is actually responsible for any difference found. Researchers have shown that gender accounts typically for only 5–10 per cent of the differences observed between individuals' behaviour (Eagly 1997). In other words, gender is a very poor predictor of behaviour, and women's and men's behaviour is much more similar than it is different. Similarities and overlaps, however, do not apparently make for publishable studies. Some academic journals have an editorial policy which excludes studies which do not find statistically significant differences, even though these differences can actually be quite small and mean very little. In ignoring overlap, what we end up doing is comparing one small section of men with one small section of women, in fact two small groups at extreme ends of a continuum. The effect of doing this is to make our research findings match our (stereotyped) characterizations.

There is worse: when results actually run counter to expectation, interpretation is used to bring results into line. Although dated, I cannot resist re-counting the following experiment, its interpretation and re-use by Jespersen in his chapter 'The Woman' in his book *Language: its nature, development and origin,* quoted in Cameron (1990: 217). Jespersen is commenting on what he considers to be the 'greater rapidity of female thought' and describes an experiment by a certain Romanes:

> The same paragraph was presented to various well-educated people, who were asked to read it as rapidly as they could, ten seconds being allowed for twenty lines. As soon as the time was up the paragraph was removed, and the reader immediately wrote down all that he or she could remember of it. It was found that women were usually more successful than men in this test. Not only were they able to read more quickly than the men, but they were able to give a better account of the paragraph as a whole. One lady, for instance, could read exactly four times as fast as her husband, and even then give a better account than he of that small portion of the paragraph he had alone been able to read. But it was found that this rapidity was no proof of intellectual power, and some of the slowest readers were highly distinguished men.

Ellis (1904: 195 in Cameron 1990: 217) explains it this way:

> with the quick reader it is as though every statement were admitted immediately and without inspection to fill the vacant chambers of the mind, while with the slow reader every statement undergoes an instinctive process of cross-examination; every new fact seems to stir up the accumulated stores of facts among which it intrudes, and so impedes rapidity of mental action.

Dale Spender, in her groundbreaking *Man Made Language* (1985) made a similar point about male bias in interpreting sex differences in the experimental setting. Witkin (1962) and his colleagues wanted to find out if women and men displayed differences in the perception of a figure in a background. Would they see the image whole, or as a separate figure and field? Finding that women tended to see the whole picture and men to separate the figure from its context, Witkin named the two perceptual patterns 'field depend-ence' and 'field independence'. Spender writes of his naming strategy:

> He took the existing patterns of male as positive and female
> as negative and objectively devised his labels. He named the
> behaviour of males as field independence, thereby perpetuating
> and strengthening the image of male supremacy; he named the
> female behaviour as field dependence and thereby perpetuated
> and strengthened the image of female inferiority.
>
> (1985: 164)

Adding that there was nothing about the results which required such discriminatory naming, Spender notes that with her bias, she could have named the perceptual tendencies as 'context aware-ness' and 'context blindness'. Neutral terms were also available: 'context awareness' and 'figure awareness'. Anne Fausto-Sterling in her book *Myths of gender* (1985) notes, regarding the test, that the experiment Witkin carried out was conducted in a pitch black room with a male experimenter, a fact she argues that could have affected women's performance. A tactile version of the test designed to measure field dependence in blind people found no sex-related differences, except in one case favouring females (1985: 31–2).

Another significant problem with sex-difference research is the common failure to use matched sampling, with the result that sta-tus or role may interfere with the identification of gender differ-ences. In a male-dominated society, status and social roles are not equally awarded to women and men; men will occupy high-status occupations and women lower ones. It is not easy then to separate out gender and status in the experimental setting.

If we decide to conduct a study on a language feature (let us say interruption and its frequency) in conversation, and we wish to test for a gender difference, we need to be careful to control for all the other variables which could have an effect on our results. Imagine that we use for informants a set of 100 pairs of office co-workers. As we want to test for male/female difference, we choose pairs who work closely together. Many of our pairs are composed of male office managers, directors and so on, and their secretaries, who are female. We tape hours of their workplace interactions. Imagine that we find that 75 per cent of interruptions were made by men and 25 per cent by women. Have we proved that men inter-rupt more than women? Possibly. The research design has not, however, used a matched sample: the women are not of the same status as the men, but are hierarchically subordinate. Our results might only be telling us that bosses interrupt secretaries more than secretaries interrupt bosses.

Moreover, how we define an interruption and what interruptions do, also needs to be addressed before we start counting them. Not all interruptions work the same way or have the same effects upon conversation (James and Clarke 1993). Research has shown also that different ethnic groups and age groups display more or less 'involved' conversational styles (Modan 1994). In some groups interruption is common, and even expected, and is interpreted as a show of interest (Tannen 1995b). Other factors we need to take into account are context (where, when interaction takes place), function (what are participants meant/trying to do), topic, relationship between speakers, frequency of interaction, lengths of conversation, and so on. All of these have effects upon people's linguistic behaviour, as indeed does individual personality. Sex-difference research will inevitably be flawed if it fails to account for factors such as these in its search for that ultimate difference.

Having cautioned against the problems in methodology and interpretation, we now turn to Chapter 6, which provides a summary of research findings highlighting issues of method.

Summary

- feminist sociolinguistics challenges the implicit male-as-norm bias in mainstream data interpretation

- how researchers conceptualize gender affects research, design and interpretation of results

- speaker sex as an explanatory variable assumes women (or men) form a homogeneous group

- feminists are not a homogeneous group, and this is reflected in the ways feminist linguists research language use

- male-as-norm bias in linguistics led to a view of women's language as deficient

- feminist work in sociolinguistics challenged stereotypes of women's language to highlight women's competence as conversationalists

- three different perspectives have emerged in feminist sociolinguistics: a dominance approach which explains linguistic behaviour in terms of gender inequality; a difference approach which focuses on re-valuing women's style; a postmodernist approach which challenges the binary opposition of gender

- research methodology needs to be refined so that other variables are controlled for in experimental settings, if we wish to test for gender difference

Further reading

Cameron, Deborah, Frazer, Elizabeth *et al.* (eds) 1992 *Researching language: issues of power and method*, Routledge, London, Introduction, pp. 5–27.

Delphy, Christine 1984 'Protofeminism or anti-feminism', in *Close to home: a materialist analysis of women's oppression*, trans. and ed. by Diana Leonard Hutchinson, London, pp. 182–210.

Aries, Elizabeth 1996 *Men and women in interaction: reconsidering the differences*, Oxford University Press, New York.

Chapter 6

Gender and language use: the evidence

Chapter outline

This chapter reviews in brief sociolinguistic research on women's and men's language styles in interaction. It will

- present the findings of sex-difference research in language from 1975 to the present
- draw attention to the research protocols and interpretations
- relate the findings to the difference and dominance frameworks
- identify similarities with findings on other social divisions such as class, role and status, raising the issue of power
- offer suggestions for a student research project and provide guidelines on methodology

There now exists a substantial literature in the field of sociolinguistics with a focus on sex difference in language use. This chapter aims to guide the interested reader through this literature by showing how it has developed since the early 1970s both in terms of research topics and of interpretations. Given the scope of this work, this chapter must necessarily present the topic in summary manner. Like any introductory textbook, this book cannot give readers what they would find by consulting some of the original work. A recent collection by Coates (1998) would make a particularly useful start for a reader who wishes to read a wide range of articles on the type of research summarized here. Other anthologies with relevant sections are Wodak (1997), Bergvall, Bing and Freed (1996), Kotthoff and Wodak (1997), Coates and Cameron (1989), Cheshire and Trudgill (1998).

Sex-difference research in language

Before outlining the research findings, I will present some different views on how to interpret the findings which have emerged. This may appear to be putting the cart before the horse. However, there can be little doubt that a researcher's views of and understanding of sex, gender and the relative positions of women and men in society, will affect how they interpret research findings and even how they conduct research. When Coates published a large study based on all-female conversation, she entitled it *Women Talk* (1996). Numerous studies based on males' speech, however, have simply omitted to mention men, boys or males from their titles. While this 'think humans for males' bias is now far less likely to be found, androcentrism in interpretation is still relatively common and manifested in attempts to explain women's use of this, that or the other form or variable in language, while assuming no need to explain men's use, viewed as the norm from which women deviate.

Work on language use and sex difference has reflected the developments in feminist and cultural studies generally. Insofar as these two bodies of theory have developed differently in Britain, Continental Europe, Canada, Australia and the United States, it is not surprising to find that work on language use and sex difference has reflected the time and the national origins of researchers. Theories which focus on power and structural factors have predominated in Britain and most of Northern Europe for example, while those focusing on difference have flourished in the USA and in France.

Views of sex and gender have altered radically since the early 1970s, affecting interpretation of data in ways which may appear confusing for a reader attempting to come to grips with this body of research. The earliest position taken up seems to have been to ignore women altogether or assume women's language use was the same as that of men. Then, in the early 1970s, sex was added as a variable like class, age and ethnic group in most variationist studies (work which attempts to correlate a linguistic variable with social differences). As feminists began to theorize gender in terms of a socially constructed difference <u>and</u> inequality, research focused on how a social group's language use reflected their powerful or powerless status, and parallels were drawn between what had been seen as women's stylistic features (Lakoff 1975) and powerless features (O'Barr and Atkins 1980). Feminist work focusing upon topic control and interruption showed that men dominated women in conversation, as they do in society at large (Zimmerman and West 1975).

The development of American cultural feminism, reinforced by the importation of (often poorly translated) French psycho-analytic feminist texts, led to a shift from a dominance approach to a difference approach and a shift towards single-sex studies. Studies focusing on women's conversational strategies have been a welcome antidote to early work which ignored, marginalized or derided women's use of language. The difference approach in its more extreme form, the dual cultures perspective (see Chapter 7), drew criticism from feminists operating with a dominance perspect-ive, especially in Europe.

These debates continue. While Holmes presents arguments for the existence of cross-cultural universals in women's linguistic habits as compared with men's in a 1993 paper (reprinted in Coates 1998), by 1997 she has shifted perspective to adopt something approaching a postmodernist position insofar as she argues for an interpretation of the story-telling narrative strategies discussed in terms of the 'doing' of femininity or masculinity. This post-modernist approach moves beyond the difference–dominance dichotomy by presenting stylistic variation as available for people to construct their identities as they choose. This position will be examined in more detail later, but we should note that, while the dominance approach attempts to integrate other social variables, especially social class, into its framework, the postmodernist line challenges *all* such categories by arguing that speakers have access to a vast array of linguistic resources which, in themselves, are multifunctional and can be interpreted in any number of ways. In Butler's words:

> There is no gender identity behind the expressions of gender; that identity is performatively constituted by the very 'expressions' that are said to be its results.
>
> (1990: 25)

In other words, gender is something that we do, not something that we have. Those sceptical of postmodernist thinking on gen-der would argue that women are not free to perform masculinity, without censure or ridicule. Bing and Bergvall (1996) quote the interesting example of a woman arrested for pumping iron in the men's weights room at her Boston gym and argue that what is at stake is not female/male difference but female/female difference. Women are not allowed to be individuals, different from one another, even in a country which bases its values on the rights of the individual. This problem lies at the heart of many interpretations of data in sex-difference research: the overlaps between women and men and differences among women or among men are minimized or denied, while female–male differences are exaggerated, especially in popularizing texts.

The remainder of this chapter will summarize and comment on sex/gender difference in language usage under three headings: phonology and grammar; lexis and pragmatic particles; discourse features. I have linked phonology and grammar because in both areas women's and men's production tends to be measured in terms of standard and non-standard variants. I have linked lexis and pragmatic particles because of wide-ranging claims that women use more of certain kinds of words (affective adjectives, adverbs) and more pragmatic particles such as hedges, tag questions and 'you know'. These could also be analysed under the grammar heading as they often involve choice of verbal forms or sentence types. They could equally be analysed under discourse, because of the functions they fill in conversation. In a sense, any division is relatively arbitrary, but I have chosen this division in order to put structure on a vast and expanding field of enquiry.

Phonology and grammar

There is almost a consensus among sociolinguists that whatever language one analyses, women and men will be found to speak differently in some way or another. This is hardly surprising when we consider that all known societies divide human beings (and other creatures) into the categories female and male and allot different status to them on this basis. Male domination appears to be a quasi-universal phenomenon, although its forms differ in time and space. Despite the fact that humans are weakly dimorphic (or rather because of the fact), differences between females and males are exaggerated and women and men created by culture. We mark gender (socially constructed differences designed to draw attention to and make sense of sex) by a wide variety of stratagems, such as the allocation of space (men get more), the design of clothing (men's is more comfortable, practical, cheaper and tends to have useful pockets) and requirements of our voices, our vocabulary, intonation and general behaviour in speech.

But surely voice at least is natural, I imagine you object. Yes and no. Voice pitch and resonance are a function of vocal tract and size and hormone levels. Nevertheless, there is mounting evidence to show that we exercise some individual control over voice production, and that we make social judgements on the basis of features of the voice. As men have lower voices than woman on average, and since we live in a society where men are valued more than women, then low voices are valued more than high-pitched voices. We are all capable of a much wider range than we actually use, which suggests that women could speak lower and men higher than we customarily do. However, men with high voices are considered effeminate and ridiculed. Women with (deliberately) low voices are given well-paid jobs as newscasters on television (Badawi), or less well-paid but prestigious ones such as Prime Minister (Thatcher). Cross-cultural studies also show that languages are spoken at different average pitches, so that, for example, if a Russian and a British speaker learn French to the point of speaking without any discernible foreign accent, the Russian will nonetheless sound more authentically French, due to the similarity of range of Russian and French measured in Hz.

Although before the onset of puberty, girls' and boys' vocal tracts are similar in size, studies have shown that it is possible to guess the sex of a child from a recording of the voice. The differences appear to be due to deliberate muscular postures called articulatory settings (Graddol and Swann 1989: 26). Deliberate manipulation of the voice by women and men may then be one of the ways in which we (are encouraged to) 'do' gender. Arguably, we 'do' other things than gender, such as sexiness (breathy voice), parental authority (shouting or menacing tone) and deference or fear (mumbling, stammering) and so on.

One of the more interesting findings on voice suggests that women use a wider intonational range than men, in other words, that women's speech is more dynamic, less monotonous than men's. I have personally noticed, as a language teacher and student, that recordings of women's voices are preferred by students taking aural examinations. Studies in phonology have also found that women tend to 'style shift' to a greater extent than men, that is women command a wider range of social styles than men and will therefore occupy more of a given continuum of variation. Variationist studies which test phonological variables as measured against social factors such as age, social class, education, gender have shown a greater degree of style-shifting among women

(Trudgill 1972). By definition, style-shifting means that a speaker is aware of the existence of more than one possible pronunciation, is capable in her or his own speech of producing more than one pronunciation and consciously (or unconsciously) does so depending on the circumstances. Most studies correlating gender with pronunciation patterns have found that women are more likely than men to use the prestige or standard form. Such patterns are gender-preferential, not gender-exclusive, that is, there is no absolute correlation between a person's speech pattern and gender identity. (See Bradley 1998 for an example of a language and society where gender-exclusive patterns are the norm.)

Moreover, not all studies have found that women adopt the standard or prestige form more than men. Many factors affect a person's choice of language, especially exposure to different varieties, employment opportunities, education, patterns of socialization, leisure activities, overt and covert cultural norms. Women in societies where boys but not girls receive secondary education or university education, will rarely acquire prestige linguistic varieties, having only access to the vernacular. The opposite situation may occur when, for example, men are farmers and women traders with wider social contacts. Employment opportunities in all societies tend to be different for women and men, since a gender division of labour is the norm: thus, market forces will often explain the development of different language norms for speakers (Nichols 1983, Cameron and Coates, 1989).

A further development of the market forces hypothesis was made by Lesley Milroy who studied three working-class communities in Belfast (Milroy 1980). Milroy found that gender could not explain the data her research produced, and employment patterning was also inadequate to account for it. She developed a model which has become known as social network analysis. This model accounts for loyalty to vernacular speech norms not by a simple dichotomous overt-versus-covert prestige hypothesis, but by reference to community norms. The more people are integrated in a community (by work, kinship and friendship ties, socializing etc.), the greater the sense of belonging, solidarity and loyalty to that community. This would include linguistic norms, as a potent symbol of membership of the community. A person's 'score' in terms of network strength would be decreased if s/he worked outside the community and strengthened if s/he worked with others from the same community. The advantage of this model is that it does not use a simplistic sex division but relies upon observable behaviours to assess linguistic loyalty. It would be useful to develop the model to remove that male bias in the criteria chosen to indicate network strength. If we use paid work in the community as a criterion, then unpaid work (housework) appears not to contribute to a person's score, as the incumbent is seen as isolated in this activity. However, one could argue that women working in the home maintain network ties when they meet in the course of typical activities such as collecting children from school, running the local youth club and even shopping.

Thomas's study (1989) in a Welsh village found evidence for the social networks hypothesis, as did Cheshire's (1982) work on adolescents in the town of Reading. Cheshire found that boys used more non-standard grammatical forms as well as pronunciations. Moreover, unlike girls, who tended to code-switch towards standard speech norms when at school, the boys maintained or even reinforced their vernacular speech habits with teachers. Such behaviour has been explained in terms of covert, masculine prestige, and has been identified by a number of researchers in a variety of countries (see James 1996 for a review). If girls code-switch to standard norms at school and boys do not, it appears that girls are accommodating their speech to that of the teacher. Eisikovits (1987) found the same process occurring when girls were interviewed by an adult female researcher; the boys in her study increased their use of stigmatized features when interviewed by the researcher. Abu-Haidar (1989) found Baghdadi men style-shifting away from prestige norms with a male interviewer, and invoked Trudgill's covert prestige notion to account for this, and a study of American college fraternity men (Kiesling 1998) also argues that men use non-standard pronunciation as part of their self-presentation as physically powerful and confrontational. While finding gender was the most salient factor in their study of variation between standard Dutch and Amsterdam vernacular, Brouwer and Van Hout (1992) also noted that high educational level, white-collar employment and being a parent increased likelihood of prestige variety forms over local dialectal forms.

The connotations of working-class dialects and accents as masculine, tough and confrontational may cause women to avoid them, given gender prescriptions on behaviour. Another reason, according to Gordon (1994) is that for women, vernacular speech forms may connote promiscuity or sexual immorality. She challenges Trudgill's view (in his early work) that women speak as they do to appear 'better' than they are, providing an alternative explanation:

> The picture of the insecure, socially climbing woman ignores some
> of the severe penalties attached to appearing lower class. Here
> I am referring not so much to social penalties as to moral ones.
> Women act in certain ways not because they want to appear
> 'better' than they really are but because they want to avoid the
> moral judgements that people make on the basis of speech and
> class stereotypes.
>
> (Gordon 1994: 217)

She goes on to argue that 'for a woman, lower-class speech forms
can also carry a possible suggestion of sexual promiscuity and loose
morals' (1994: 218), citing as evidence adolescent boys' judgements
of the tape-recorded voices of two women, one vernacular and one
standard speaker of New Zealand English.

This observation and other research (for example, Gal 1979,
Eckert and McConnell-Ginet 1995, McElhinny 1998) raise the issue
of the relationships between language use and identity. Although
the issue of agency is now hotly contested (Fairclough 1992, Butler
1990, Lee 1992), a compelling argument has been made to claim
that speakers actively construct their identities in speaking, precisely by choosing language forms which carry social connotations
in line with their beliefs, loyalties, aspirations and so on. Clearly,
speakers choose among the available varieties to which they have
been exposed, and which have been determined by socio-historical
and economic factors. For example, in North Africa, speakers may
opt to speak French, English, educated forms of standard Arabic
or local vernacular varieties; in Wales, Welsh or English; in South
Carolina, standard American English or Gullah (Nichols 1983).
In such situations of code choice, speakers' choices may depend
on a wide variety of factors. Dhaouadi (1996) argues that Tunisian
women's pronunciation of 'r' represents an act of identity based
on imitation of a modernist Western model of femininity, an interpretation which could be contested from a feminist perspective.
Gal's work on a diglossic Austrian community (Gal 1979) showed
that women's choice of standard Austrian German over the local
Hungarian vernacular constituted an act of identity which could
be summarized as a rejection of peasant wife status and espousal
of more egalitarian norms associated with use of German and more
urban lifestyles.

Nor do women and girls systematically opt for the standard or
prestige form. Sensitivity to codes and their connotations encourages
successful code-switching. Eckert and McConnell-Ginet's (1995)
work on 'burnouts' and 'jocks' in Belten High School shows that

girls performed their jock or burnout status more convincingly than boys, that is that jock girls used more jock linguistic features than jock boys and burnout girls conformed more than male counterparts to burnout linguistic forms. It could be argued that to be taken seriously at anything, girls need to outperform boys.

In conclusion, research shows that despite the quasi-consensus on differences between women's and men's speech, a note of caution should be sounded. Women do not always opt for the standard form and men the non-standard; sometimes the reverse occurs. Moreover, speakers do not always adopt the same form, but style-shift or code-shift as they deem appropriate. Given this potential flexibility, it seems clear that it is unsatisfactory to conduct research which, from the outset, expects a gender difference and is designed to find one. More nuanced models are necessary, models which would not divide speakers into two polarized groups each of which is viewed as fixed and homogeneous. The dichotomous sex-difference model is nowhere more evident than in early work on lexis and pragmatic particles, to which we now turn.

Lexis and pragmatic particles

We cannot underestimate the importance of Lakoff's 1975 publication *Language and woman's place*. Even if it has been roundly criticized by feminists since, in particular for its methodology (intro-spection/speaker intuition), this work acted as a catalyst for the vast language and gender research which followed. This is no more the case than in explorations of women's and men's vocabularies (lexis) and use of pragmatic particles such as tag questions, hedging expressions (sort of, kind of), modal verb forms and adverbs (may, might, could, possibly, perhaps) and the phrase 'you know'. These linguistic features have been singled out for particular attention in research since Lakoff's claim that women's speech tended to be full of such expressions and forms, since they are a reflection of women's subordinate status. Lakoff's claims regarding lexis included the assertion that women use fewer swear words or 'bad' language, less slang, more 'empty' and affective adjectives and that they command a far greater range of colour terms. Because she relied upon her own intuition and observation of women in her own social circle, later researchers deliberately designed empirical research protocols, including work done in laboratory settings, to test her assertions.

Colour terms

Any discussion of lexis will bring us back to our discussion in Part 1 about language and culture. If it could be proved that women and men possessed, let us say, vastly different vocabularies of colour terms, what could we conclude? Tests of perceptual ability would show that we are all equally capable of fine distinction between colours, so we would know that the development of a greater vocabulary in one group was not natural, given, or innate. How could we explain it? We could argue that the life-worlds of women and men were different enough to warrant a greater need on the part of women for an expanded range of colour terms. In other words, might there be areas of experience typical of women's lives as prescribed by our culture which require fine discrimination of colour terms, while such a need is absent from men's lives? Perhaps an interest in fashion, fabrics, dressmaking, embroidery or interior design predispose a speaker to develop a large number of colour terms. Water-colourists of all persuasions use terms the non-artist rarely if ever does: ultramarine, burnt umber, raw sienna, alizarin crimson, cobalt blue. When I recently asked for advice in a paint store, the (male) assistant suggested that the best complement for navy soft furnishings and a maple floor would be 'wet sand' or 'Tuscany', and many will remember the merriment at the new away jersey for, I think, Liverpool Football Club, which the press described as 'écru': I would argue that, at the time, the use of this elaborate colour term in the context of football viewed as a quintessentially masculine pursuit and a dominant symbol of 'laddism', constituted an anomaly. 'Real men' had to be seen to laugh at the word, because culturally it is seen as effeminate for men to be interested in such terms. In a sense, once anything is associated with women, it becomes taboo for men and an immediate potential sign of homosexuality. Hence, Almodóvar's use of elaborate colour terms for his male characters, in his playful deconstruction of masculine identity.

Research on colour term recognition and use has confirmed Lakoff's intuition that women know, recognize and use a larger linguistic palette (Swaringen *et al.* 1978, Nowaczyk 1982, Simpson and Tarrant 1991, Yang 1996). Most of these studies have been based on college students and native speakers of English, though Yang has worked on Chinese, and has noted cross-cultural differences in the degree of variation between female and male subjects in China and in English-speaking societies. Other variables which affect performance in such tests are age, level of education, background (rural or urban) and, to my mind most significantly, whether subjects engage in colour-related hobbies such as art, or not. Yang, for example, found that ability on tests was correlated with speakers' involvement in colour-related hobbies, and noted that men were less likely than women to have such hobbies (Yang 1996: 218). Once again then, we find that while gender does appear to be a salient influence upon linguistic behaviour, it is difficult to separate it from other variables, in this case from the effect of socialization, experiential or cultural factors. Readers may like to conduct experiments of their own to test for colour lexicon.

Box 6.1 Colour names elicitation

Exercise

The aim of this exercise is to elicit as many colour terms as possible in a given time (say ten minutes). Prepare a questionnaire to be handed out immediately after the test, to append to each subject's answer sheet when completed. Go through the stages in the same order for each group of subjects. Do not vary the instructions or the time allowed, and do not answer any questions until after the experiment is complete.

1. Prepare a large lined sheet, with numbers 1 to 100 arranged in columns with enough space for subjects to write in colour names.
2. Write or record the following instructions and play, read or hand them out to subjects prior to administration of the test sheet:

> This is an experiment designed to compare the most commonly used words for colours in English with those of other languages. To make it more exciting, we are presenting it as a test, a competition. We would like you to write as many different colour words as possible in the time available, that is ten minutes, on the numbered sheet on your desk. You may turn it over when you hear the signal to start. You must stop writing as soon as you are asked to. Your sheet will be collected, then we'll give you a short questionnaire to fill in, with questions about yourself. You need not write your name: this is an anonymous test. Please do not talk during the test. Questions are not allowed. Any colour terms are

allowed including terms using more than one word. May we begin?

3. Using a stop-watch, give the signal to begin.
4. After ten minutes, give the signal to end.
5. Collect the test sheets, numbering them in sequence as you do so, if you have not already done so.
6. Hand out the questionnaire. Depending on your informants, you may wish to ask the following:

- age
- level of education
- sex
- regional background
- occupation
- hobbies, present and past

You may also wish to ask subjects to assess their own colour vocabulary as above average, average or below average. You may like to check for beliefs about colour terms. You could ask if subjects believe there may be differences according to sex, occupation, age, regional origin, nationality, involvement in hobbies.

7. Collect questionnaires, numbering them in sequence, and append them to the colour list sheet for each subject.
8. Debrief the subjects as to the aims of the research. Apologize for deceiving them, explaining the value of tacit research. Ask if anyone would now like not to be included in the experiment and return their sheet and questionnaire to them. Thank everyone, including anyone who declined to be involved.
9. Count the number of terms cited, checking against duplication, deleted terms and so on. Write the score on top of the questionnaire.
10. Depending on sample size, correlate scores with all the demographic variables by hand or using a social sciences statistical package.
11. Write up your experiment and results and present them to class-mates, if you have such an opportunity.

You may like to do some follow-up work. Read some of the articles in this research area or repeat your experiment in a different setting, or on native speakers of some other language, or on bilinguals to see if differences emerge. Revisit your results and check for overlap rather than difference, if it was difference you measured. Ask yourself why you did not check for overlap!

Box 6.2 Colour naming

Exercise

The aim of this exercise is to test subjects' ability to use elaborate colour terms for colours which are outside the focal range. Again, you may use the questionnaire used in Box 6.1 to correlate results with social variables. The time needed for this experiment will depend upon the number of colour chips you use, but thirty seconds per colour should suffice. This experiment needs to be done in a room with good light so that all subjects have good conditions for seeing the colours. It is unlikely that readers will have access to an ophthalmologist to test for colour vision deficiency beforehand. Bear this in mind in making any claims for your data.

1. Prepare a bright room to accommodate your subjects.
2. Using paint-store colour chips, prepare a sheet of colours with numbers but not names, leaving room between them for subjects to write in names, or use the one provided at the end of Chapter 3. Number the sheets on the reverse to keep track of your informants' answers, for appending to the ensuing demographics questionnaire.
3. Record and play or read out the following instructions:

   Thank you for agreeing to take part in this English language study about colour vocabulary. We would like you to name, as precisely as possible, the colours on the sheet before you. Please write the name you have chosen beside each colour in the space available. There are no right or wrong answers, as colour naming is quite subjective. You will be allowed X minutes to complete the sheet, then we will collect them and ask you to fill in a simple, anonymous questionnaire. May we begin? Please do not talk or ask questions.

4. Give signal to begin.
5. Give signal to stop. Collect test sheets in sequence.
6. Distribute demographics questionnaire, as in Exercise 1.
7. Collect and append questionnaires to colour test sheets.
8. Debrief your subjects as per Exercise 1.
9. Score the colour-naming exercise. Clearly, this could be subjective, so it would be better to use several judges and establish agreed criteria beforehand. For example, if you select a very dark shade of green as one chip, you may score as follows:

| Blue | 0 | Dark green | 2 |
| Green | 1 | Bottle green | 3 |

You will need to decide what to do if people 'invent' colour terms, e.g. pine-needle green or use idiosyncratic colour terms with only local connotations, e.g. 'Ogmore Grammar School sock red', or 'Real Madrid away jersey purple'.

10. Correlate scores with social variables.
11. Write up your results and present to your class-mates, if applicable.

You may like to do some further work. Read some of the relevant research on colour perception and naming (Berlin and Kay 1969, Rosch 1975). Using the same colour sheet, test speakers of other languages, as well as bilinguals and second-language learners. Try the test on people of different age ranges and occupations. Remember to check for overlap as well as difference. Revisit your data and check to see what domains terms are drawn from, e.g. food colours (cinnamon, turmeric, pistachio, melon); gardening colours (daffodil yellow, clematis Montana rubens pink, chestnut); foreign language borrowings (écru, taupe, beige, citron) and whether these domains are age, sex or region related.

We now turn to an area of lexis where men are thought to outdo women, swearing.

Swearing

Compare the following:

1. The prevailing atmospheric conditions could have serious physiological consequences upon the lower appendages of small, simulated, simian creatures, constructed of an alloy of copper and zinc.
   'It's cold enough to freeze the balls off a brass monkey!'
2. Go forth and multiply.
   'Fuck off'.

Most cultures, and thus most languages, have words which are considered taboo. As we saw in Chapters 3 and 4, taboos vary from culture to culture. In English-speaking Western cultures, swearing involves taboo reference to our animal nature, our sexual nature and to religion, in other words to the liminal states of (sub) humanity and (super) humanity, seen from the point of view of the human as culturally made. Swear words in our culture are those which remind us that we are animals and that we are not gods.

Swear words are not appropriate for all communication settings, and are not considered equally appropriate for all speakers. When I ask first-year languages undergraduates to list three pet linguistic hates, swearing systematically tops the list, and children swearing is the extreme case for these students. Early research identified swearing, slang and coarse expressions as a masculine prerogative. Jespersen (1964 [1922]) and Lakoff (1975) both claimed that women avoided such expressions. Swearing and slang would be considered as the lexical form of non-standard language, akin to 'I done it' for 'I did it' and non-standard pronunciation of -ing words.

A number of feminist studies have disputed that knowledge of and use of such taboo words are a feature of men's language as opposed to women's. Once again, methodological issues have been relevant to the stereotyped view of women's language. It has been argued that speakers are less likely to admit to knowing or using such terms to an interviewer (Zajonc 1962, quoted in Risch 1987). This is likely to be most acute when the interviewer is of a different generation, or gender or social class. Risch describes an experiment designed to elicit from female linguistics and composition students taboo terms they and their friends use to refer to men. Interviewers chosen were female and themselves uttered some such words by way of example and to reduce apprehension about producing such terms. Fifty different terms were elicited, which Risch grouped by metaphorical classification (birth, ass, head, dick, boys, animal, meat, other). It is worth noting that a very similar metaphorical process is at work in men's derogatory terms for women (Schultz [1975] 1990), and in American college students' terms for the penis (Cameron 1992a).

Risch found that, contrary to beliefs that women tend to use more standard forms of speech, her middle-class informants admitted to using taboo terms. She emphasizes the importance of setting and interviewer sex in eliciting use of taboo words to reduce observer paradox effects, noting also that the function of such taboo may be to mark solidarity (just as slang marks intergenerational boundaries). She cautions that taboo language may actually carry covert prestige for young women, a point which reinforces Trudgill's own, early findings that young women, like men of all ages, were more likely to opt for non-standard features. In postmodernist terms, we could argue that young (and not so young) women may be using taboo language precisely not to 'do femininity' as prescriptively given.

Work elsewhere has confirmed Risch's findings. A study on South-African adolescents (De Klerk 1992) found that girls knew more slang terms than boys and that specifically, they knew and used more anti-male terms. It was not gender, however, but age, which had the most significant effect upon response rates. Again, De Klerk's students were largely middle class, showing that swearing or knowledge of taboo words is neither a working class nor a male phenomenon. A study focusing on working-class women in Ordsall, Salford, a deprived inner-city area in England (Hughes 1992), found that swear words and taboo language were 'an integral part of their language' (1992: 297). Hughes agrees with Coates and Cameron (1989: 23) that there is little or no incentive for these women to use standard English. Contrary to claims that swearing is used to shock middle-class people, Hughes found it to be used to children (cf: Brouwer and Van Hout 1992) and to close friends, though not to parents. Hughes concludes:

> The women of Ordsall Family Center are not breaking any language 'rules' that prescribe that women use more standard speech, more euphemisms, that they be more linguistically polite and use less slang and expletives than men. They are merely using *their* language, *their* norm; it is a norm that appears to be virtually unaccounted for in sociolinguistic studies. They are exhibiting a branch of 'female speech' that is perfectly in keeping with their class, economic situation, and social network structure.
>
> (1992: 300)

Once again, findings in this area lead to the conclusion that gender cannot be isolated for use as an explanatory variable. It cannot be emphasized enough that when speaking, a person's sex or gender is only one (unfixed) factor in the total communication context. We speak to another, in a specific context, with particular aims in mind. A good research model for anyone who wishes to discover if there are differences between women's and men's speech patterns would need to control for every single other variable (setting, purpose, as well as demographics and status/role considerations). Recent research on pragmatic particles has aimed to do just that, with the result that early, classic work in the field has now been challenged for methodological and interpretative bias. Specifically, the focus has been on the need to control for interfering variables, and to be aware of the differing functions a linguistic form may play.

Pragmatic particles

In its most comprehensive sense, pragmatics is that part of linguistics which accounts for the very general underlying principles which speakers follow when engaging with others in communication. Consider the following snatches of conversation:

1. Anne: Hi Jane, are you going to the beach?
   Jane: I've got a dental appointment at eleven.
2. Anne: Hi Jane, are you going to the beach?
   Jane: It *is* a nice day, isn't it?
3. Anne: Hi Jane, are you going to the beach?
   Jane: My car's in for a service.

On the face of it, Jane's response does not seem like an appropriate response in any of the examples. Yet, we can imagine such responses routinely given to such questions. Listeners can usually assume that speakers are genuinely engaged in conversation, and are speaking with the intent to be understood. Pragmatics attempts to understand what the underlying rules are in speakers' attempts to understand utterances. In example one above, Anne understands that Jane is not going to the beach; in example two, Jane responds as if Anne's question were a cross between a question and a suggestion. Her reply shows that she might consider going to the beach. In example three, the 'world knowledge' of Anne is involved: Jane and Anne know that you need a car to go the beach, Jane's car is unavailable, therefore Jane will not be going to the beach. This conversation might continue:

Anne: Hi Jane, are you going to the beach?
Jane: My car's in for a service.
Anne: Oh well, do you want to come with us? We're going around two.

These examples have aimed to show that conversation <u>ideally</u> involves cooperation between speakers. Grice (1957) attempted to outline the principles or maxims of co-operation underlying interaction, proposing the following four:

- Maxim of quantity (don't be too brief or too longwinded).
- Maxim of quality (be truthful).
- Maxim of relevance (reply appropriately given the context, speaker's utterance etc.).
- Maxim of manner (be clear, try not to confuse the hearer).

Research on naturally occurring conversation has shown that not all speakers apply such principles in practice. The simple idea that conversation involves taking turns and that there is a preferred response to particular utterances (question–answer, invitation–acceptance; apology–minimization), so called adjacency pairs (Sacks *et al.* 1974) has, in practice, been shown to be a little idealistic. Early feminist work on discourse structure suggested that while women tended to be co-operative in conversation, men tended to be competitive. We will review this in the following section, on discourse, and in Chapter 7.

At this point, we can examine what have been termed pragmatic particles, features of spoken language identified early by Lakoff (1975) as typical of women's conversational style. According to Lakoff, pragmatic particles feature greatly in women's language because they carry or connote lack of authority, deference to the other speaker, hesitancy and conversational insecurity. Working from a dominance paradigm, Lakoff put this down to women's subordinate social position and their socialization. Later, in the 1980s, when women's 'difference' came to be celebrated, features like tag questions, hedges and so on were reinterpreted as positive contributions to women's distinctive co-operative style. We will focus here on the tag question and the use of 'you know', as these are the most developed in the feminist literature.

According to Lakoff the tag question can be used legitimately to check information, as in 'Croatia beat Holland 2–1 in the play-offs, *didn't they?*'; or illegitimately to ask the hearer for confirmation of the speaker's own viewpoint or feeling, as in 'It's cold in here, *isn't it?*' Lakoff considered that women avoided direct statements of opinion and used tag questions to add a level of tentativeness to assertions. Critics of Lakoff's position reviewed the function of tag questions and argued against her position, which they felt reinforced the notion that women's language was in some way deficient.

Holmes (1986) argued against Lakoff that the second kind of tag, Lakoff's illegitimately used tag, ought to be seen in pragmatic terms as hearer-oriented, for example, as inviting the hearer to respond. Tags can work to invite the hearer into conversation, and do not necessarily convey lack of authority or conviction. Tags can also be used to soften or mitigate the strength of a criticism. A teacher might say to a pupil: 'You didn't do much preparation really, *did you?*' order to reduce the face-threatening (Brown and Levinson 1978) impact of a direct accusation. A tag in such a position invites the hearer to agree, in other words involves the negotiation of a shared interpretation of events. Tags can thus be seen as one of a range of politeness strategies aimed at face maintenance for addressees. In her 1986 article on the functions of *you know* in speech, Holmes noted that while there was no difference in the frequency of *you know* between female and male speakers, women's and men's usage differed according to the function *you know* played in their speech. According to Holmes, women use more facilitative expressions, and men more modal tags. Women's facilitative expressions convey the speaker's positive attitude to the addressee, her solidarity with interlocutors and invite collaboration in discourse. Men are less likely to use such features. Holmes points out the methodological bias in early attempts to confirm or disprove Lakoff's assertions. Hedges and tag questions were often simply counted and taken to be representative of 'women's language' (Holmes 1986: 4). The actual function played by the particular form was often ignored, as was general context or setting and even a check on the occurrence of the features in question as measured against total 'amount of talk'. Holmes's own examination of *you know* compares women's and men's production of the feature according to its position in the sentence and its function. *You know* can function to raise a topic, to express confidence, to express uncertainty, to emphasize the speech act or to introduce a rephrasing when a speaker hesitates over word choice or changes tack mid-sentence. Her data challenge Lakoff's reading of 'women's language' forms as women in Holmes's study were as likely to use *you know* to express certainty as doubt. She argues:

> The analysis of the function of particular occurrences of *you know* requires that careful account be taken not only of linguistic features such as intonation and syntactic position, but also of the illocutionary point of the particular speech act in the discourse, the purpose and degree of formality of interaction, the relative statuses and role of participants, and the amount of shared background knowledge and experience they can assume.
>
> (Holmes 1986: 17)

Contrary to both Lakoff's and Holmes's position, researchers working on asymmetrical discourse, that is talk between speakers who are positioned by the institutional setting to be highly differentiated socially (doctor–patient, defendant–magistrate etc.), have found that tags may be used by powerful speakers to express power over hearers. Harris (1984) quoted by Cameron (1992b: 19) gives a good example:

'You're not making much effort to pay off these arrears, *are you?*'

A psychiatrist of my acquaintance addressed a girl-friend of her drug-addicted patient thus:

'You're not going to stay with this loser, *are you?*'

Both these examples illustrate how tags can function to perform power in interaction. Even though both these examples are question forms inviting a hearer to contribute to the talk, they can hardly be said to convey the same effect as the tag in

'It's cold in here, *isn't it?*'

The tag questions of powerful speakers are relatively conducive of particular answers. The magistrate's question is rhetorical, and acts as an observation. The psychiatrist's is a challenge, in effect telling the girl-friend to leave her addicted lover. Thus, tag questions, like *you know*, express a range of attitudes, and help to position speakers relative to one another. Thus, speaker gender is likely to be far too simplistic an explanatory variable in studies of conversation.

Freed and Greenwood (1996) found exactly that in their study of dyadic conversations between eight same-sex pairs of friends. They recorded speakers engaged in three different kinds of talk which the researchers elicited by careful manipulation of the setting: spontaneous talk prior to the 'official' recording; considered talk with a set topic; and collaborative talk, recorded while the subjects filled out a questionnaire. The researchers found no female–male difference in frequency of questions or use of *you know*, nor in the functions these features have in speech. They did find, however, that type of talk (in other words task-orientation) determined the use of pragmatic particles and questions. Having adjusted their figures for time of each segment or type of talk, Freed and Greenwood found that 89 per cent of occurrences of *you know* occurred during the second part of the experiment, that is during the considered talk, when the pairs of friends were asked to discuss the nature of friendship between women compared to men's friendship. Their findings represent a strong counter argument to the dual cultures perspective which argues for different female and male sub-cultural norms for conversation. It was not gender, but function of interaction which determined the use of the pragmatic features.

This necessarily brief discussion has shown that the interpretation given to a particular linguistic feature within the context of sex/gender and language research depends largely on the researcher's prior understanding of gender. The dominance perspective seems to downplay women's resistance to gender hierarchy (inequality); the difference perspective reinforces sex stereotyping, albeit by celebrating women's conversational competence. Cameron makes a plea for a different kind of research protocol:

> Instead of searching for the linguistic correlates of these monoliths [women's and men's language] then, we might proceed by asking slightly different questions – questions about how language is being used, by real people in real situations, to *construct* gender and gender relations. So when women and men employ particular linguistic forms and strategies, how are these heard and used to reproduce or subvert social relations between the sexes?
>
> (1992b: 24)

This is a question to bear in mind in looking at the last section of this chapter, discourse. This topic has been researched in more detail than any other. The presentation given here is by necessity a brief one. Readers in this area can gain a deeper overview by reading a number of comprehensive review articles on the various topics, referenced throughout the following summary.

Discourse

The term 'discourse' is used in a number of disciplines to refer to a variety of concepts. As far as our discussion is concerned here, the term is being used to refer to more or less lengthy occasions of public or private talk, usually with two or more speakers. Feminist interest in this field has ranged widely in terms of settings or contexts. Early work in the field focused on public settings such as classrooms (Sarah 1980) and faculty meetings (Edelsky 1981) while recent work has examined talk by women in male-dominated professions (McElhinny 1998, West 1998). However, the greater proportion of feminist work on discourse has focused on informal conversation in private settings. A variety of discourse features has been examined, often depending upon the identity of the speakers under scrutiny. Early work within the dominance framework examined cross-sex talk to identify how men silenced and subordinated women in conversation. A 1975 paper by Zimmerman and West is a classic in this paradigm, and focuses on interruptions. Later work looked at same-sex conversation, especially that between women. Dual cultures perspective research focused on miscommunication in cross-sex pairs and at work (see Chapter 7). This section will focus on a small number of features to introduce the field: topic and silencing, amount of talk, interruption, politeness, the notion of holding the conversation 'floor'.

The gender division of labour underlies the differential access of women and men to opportunities for powerful public discourse. Women are hugely under-represented in a wide range of occupations and professions which by their nature confer upon incumbents the power to hold forth, at length, virtually uninterrupted: the priesthood, academia, the legal profession and political office spring to mind. Until recently, women were rarely employed as newscasters, radio journalists or television presenters. There has been some change in these areas, but less than often imagined: a myth of progress prevents recognition of the continued marginalization of women in high paying jobs.

As a result of this division of labour, it is often difficult to determine, as a researcher, if the pattern one discerns as a gender pattern is indeed that, or if status explains one's results. We need to remember that gender is not (just) a system of difference but a system of inequality. In an institutional setting such as a court, a doctor's surgery, or a classroom, a person's gender will often be reinforced or contradicted by their status or role. It has been argued (Reynolds 1998) that women in positions of authority in Japan experience 'status conflict', reflected in speech norms. This occurs in situations where a woman is superior in status to a male interlocutor, and also when in interaction with an equal. Speech norms for women, stressing deference, humility and politeness, clash with speech norms for enacting authority (1998: 302). West has argued that gender continues to override status, and that, for example, female doctors are interrupted by patients (West 1984) while male doctors are the interrupters in patient–doctor encounters.

Topic

Just as women have been considered to possess a wide colour vocabulary because colour terms are 'trivial', so too women have been derided for topics of conversation, such as fashion, housework, shopping and other people's relationships, also viewed as trivial. Interestingly, if men talk about such topics, it is as experts and the topics become serious: fashion designers, advertising voice-over experts on washing-up-liquids, shopping programme hosts and psychologists may hold forth on these same topics with impunity. It is difficult to see how talk about football, darts or car engine performance can possibly appear less trivial than talk about relationships.

Kipers (1987) conducted empirical research to ascertain whether women and men differed in their topics of conversation in mixed and single-sex groups and whether the conversants agreed or differed on the relative importance or triviality of the topics. Her subjects were occupationally homogeneous and all conversations were taped in the staffroom of the middle-school in New Jersey where they worked as teachers. She found that women spoke more of home and family than men and less of leisure and recreation, an unsurprising finding given the typical division of labour in the home. As for triviality or otherwise of the various topics, Kipers reports general agreement on most topics. One interesting finding concerned the way conversants picked up or dropped a potential topic according to the gender composition of the group: a compliment regarding clothing addressed to a conversant would not lead to a discussion about clothes in a mixed gender group as it might in a women-only group. Kipers found, nevertheless, that all topics 'succeeded'. Topics succeed when interlocutors pick up and elaborate on subjects raised by another, said to initiate the topic. Kiper's results on this subject are not reflected in the literature reporting topic control among married couples (Fishman 1983, Spender 1985, DeFrancisco 1991). While women make huge efforts to keep conversation going, doing what Fishman calls conversational 'shitwork', these efforts are often unrewarded. Women's topics, according to such research, fail more often than men's. Women, like children, have been shown to use more attention-seeking opening gambits such as 'D'you know what?' or 'Guess what happened today' or 'You'll never believe who I saw today.' Such formulations challenge the interlocutor to reply with a question, such as 'What?' or 'Who?' This response, being a question, elicits the preferred response, an answer. Thus, the woman (or child) has been given the floor, given permission to speak.

Difference perspective researchers, focusing on women's conversational style, have shown that women use a lot of minimal responses, called backchannelling, to indicate active listening. Feminist research suggests that such expressions, like 'mm, hmm', are not used to the same extent by men. Indeed, research has shown that men use silence to silence women. Such research is normally based upon the turn-taking model of conversation (Sacks *et al.* 1974). Within the model, speakers are viewed as having a right to take a turn at a transition relevance point (i.e. when the interlocutor has finished a point, or invites the next speaker to contribute, for example, by asking a question). But speakers not only have a right to speak, they also have an obligation to speak. Lengthy pauses are avoided; listening skills are well-honed when speakers take turns without violation like interruption or delayed responses. Allowing no opportunity to the interlocutor to intervene is another obvious violation used by speakers who are fond of lecturing.

DeFrancisco's research used a number of indicators to signal successful and unsuccessful topics: responses which shut off an attempted topic; frequent interruptions; minimal, delayed or no response to topic; increases in pauses and verbalized pauses by speaker whose topic was 'in trouble' (DeFrancisco 1991: 416). Since early models for interpreting interaction have been considered too subjective and limited (for example, interruption can show involvement and interest in the topic rather than a violation and attempt to 'steal' the floor), DeFrancisco sought subjects' own interpretations of some of the episodes she recorded in the homes of the couples investigated. She played back extracts to both partners and asked for their comments. One husband commented on a 12.5 minute conversation in which he made eighteen turn-taking violations, including leaving the room to feed the dog, that he had 'heard it all before'. His wife had raised seven topics of which two had failed; he raised four, successfully. DeFrancisco concludes that women did work harder at conversation and that men's conversational behaviour could often be seen as conflict avoidance strategies, such as avoiding sensitive topics, using no-response to indicate lack of interest, talking less, and using patronizing behaviours. (1991: 419) Women complained that their husbands talked to them in teacher mode, for example. Clearly, such strategies reflect a lack of equality in relationships.

In order to attempt to separate role/status and gender, a good deal of work has been carried out on topic control in asymmetrical settings, such as doctor–patient consultations. Ainsworth-Vaughn (1992) studied topic-transitions in such encounters, comparing female and male doctors. All patients were women. She argues that gender and role prescriptions clash for female professionals, that is in this case, as a doctor, the women are expected to adopt an expert style, but as women they are expected to be cooperative or deferential. Like West (1984, 1998), Ainsworth-Vaughn found that status is over-ridden by gender. Male doctors made more abrupt changes of topic, while women negotiated topic change with the patient. Rather than viewing women's conversational behaviour as deficient, it appears to make more sense to argue for men to adopt similar styles, at least as far as doctors are concerned: patients reported more satisfaction with female doctors, and were more likely to comply with doctor's recommendations for treatment. Larger-scale studies need to be conducted, I believe, in order to control for age, sex and class as patient, as well as age and experience of physician. Ethnicity also plays a role in conversational style: some ethnic groups use high-involvement styles, while others are more subdued. I would argue that Kiper's finding that all topics succeeded in her study can be explained by the norms for middle-class academics of equal status. Outside the workplace, at a pub or a dinner party, different norms might apply. Accommodation to implicit norms varies according to composition of the group (Giles and Powesland 1975, Reid 1995).

Amount of talk

Topic of talk is not unrelated to amount of talk. Studies on amount of talk which compare women's and men's contribution to conversation in mixed-sex dyads or larger groups have yielded inconsistent results. Some studies have shown that men speak more, some that men speak more in certain circumstances, some show no gender difference, and a tiny minority (3.6 per cent) show women speak more than men (James and Drakich 1993). As with other topics, then, it appears that gender alone is not a satisfactory predictor of amount of talk. James and Drakich's meta-analysis of sixty-three studies conducted between 1951 and 1991 sought to explain why findings were inconsistent. One reason adduced for the inconsistency was difference in methodology and measurement. Amount of talk can be measured in minutes and seconds, number and length of turns at talk, number of words or number of sentences, number of speech acts, average turn length or some combination. The studies reviewed in this meta-analysis varied as to measurement method employed.

Another significant factor which influenced amount of talk was type of talk. As we saw in the previous section, the use of *you know* was influenced by task orientation, not gender, in the study conducted by Freed and Greenwood (1996). The third most significant factor James and Drakich identified was status or role of participants. Type of talk (formal, task-oriented; informal, socioemotionally driven) and relative status of participants (expert vs. non-expert; equals vs. non-equals) interact with gender to confer greater or lesser speaking rights on individuals in specific interactional contexts. Interaction is affected by how individuals rate themselves relative to co-participants and according to social expectations of oneself and others. Sex, race, ethnicity, age, class and organizational role cross-cut each other in these calculations. Needless to say, being a woman connotes low status within this paradigm. This may be offset by expert status as determined by position in an occupational hierarchy or by knowledge about the topic at hand. Thus, women are thought likely to talk more than men in an experimental setting where participants are requested to discuss knitting and sewing patterns, and less if the assigned topic is how to lay a patio.

Recent research on electronic communication (newsgroups) has suggested that differences found in spoken interaction also appear in computer-mediated discourse. Not only do women bring norms of politeness and cooperative interaction to the medium, while men seem happy to 'flame', but also an unstated limit appears to be placed by some men on women's posting to shared discussion (Herring et al. 1995). This limit is somewhat less than a fair share, or 50 per cent. As Spender had noted earlier (1985), when women constitute 30 per cent of a mixed group, the general perception is that they are fairly represented. Similarly, with talk or internet posting, if women do actually take up their fair share of 'talking time', they are perceived in fact to be dominating talk. This unstated implicit 'rule' may be one factor accounting for men's tendency to interrupt women.

Interruptions

Research on interruption has, like research on amount of talk, been inconsistent. Linguists use the everyday term interruption rather than a technical term, and this appears to suggest that the word enjoys an agreed meaning and that interruption can be researched without difficulty. Like tag questions, however, interruptions do not always have the same effect in a conversation: they can perform a variety of functions, be responded to in a number of different ways by the interrupted speaker and be interpreted differently according to the type of 'floor' being developed (Ahrens 1997, Edelsky 1981).

Box 6.3 Gender and interruption

Early work on gender and interruption was based in the dominance framework. Barely a single article about interruption fails to quote a now-famous example of a conversation between a woman and a man involving repeated turn-taking violations, first cited by Zimmerman and West (1975). In the following transcription, = symbolizes latching, (#) means a silence of one second or less, and [indicates overlapping speech:

Female: how's your paper coming? =
Male: = alright I guess.
Male: (#) I haven't done much in the past two weeks
         (1.8 seconds).
Female: Yeah, know how that ⌈ can
Male   ⌊ hey, ya' got an extra
Male: cigarette?
         (#)
Female: Oh uh sure ((hands him the pack)) like my
Female: ⌈ pa
Male: ⌊ thanks
         (1.8 seconds)
Female: Sure (#) I was gonna tell you ⌈ my –
Male: ⌊ Hey I'd really
Male: like to talk but I gotta run (#) see ya.
Female: Yeah. (Zimmerman and West 1975)

Zimmerman and West compared interruptions in same-sex and mixed-sex dyads. They found that overlaps and interruptions were shared more or less equally in same-sex dyads, but not in mixed-sex dyads. Of forty-eight interruptions in conversations between eleven mixed-sex pairs, forty-six were made by men and two by women. Only seven interruptions in total were made in twenty same-sex dyads. Such findings clearly suggest that women's speaking-rights are violated by men. (See Coates 1993: 110 for more discussion)

Feminists working within the difference or sub-cultural paradigm have pointed out that not all interruptions constitute an attempt to dominate or take the floor. Coates (1989) and Tannen (1990) argue that the Sacks, Schegloff and Jefferson turn-taking model (1974) fails to account for the more informal, collaborative talk production of intimates engaged in conversations which display conviviality, involvement and emotional connection or solidarity.

Ahrens (1997) calls for a more nuanced classification of interruptions and for more attention to be paid to the contribution of specific interruptions to the conversation as a whole and to dominance relations.

Although many researchers concur with early dominance theorists that men interrupt women far more than vice versa (Rosenblum 1986, Aries 1987, Holmes 1995) a review by James and Clarke in Tannen (1993) argued that the evidence does not support this assertion, as most studies found no difference between the genders in the number of interruptions initiated. Once again, the studies are not always strictly comparable from a methodological point of view, as different measures of interruption have been used as well as different settings (formal vs. informal; naturalistic vs. laboratory based). Virtually all studies have been conducted in English-speaking countries. Some studies have not controlled for sex of speaker being interrupted. Few controlled for type of talk, task-orientation or degree of intimacy of interlocutors.

It appears that speakers react differently to examples of interruption depending on the type of 'floor' being developed. Interruptions are noticed and resented more in formal, task-oriented, one-speaker-at-a-time floors, such as in meetings. In such contexts, it is not uncommon for interrupted speakers to counter-interrupt and signal displeasure, implicitly acknowledging the turn-taking norm. However, in a jointly or collaboratively developed floor, simultaneous speech is not viewed negatively nor as constituting interruption (Edelsky 1981). On the contrary, it is often in such a floor that speakers have the most conversational fun: joke-telling, story-telling and banter involve interruption almost by definition. Clearly the Sacks *et al.* (1974) turn-taking model of conversation cannot be applied to what Irish people call 'craic', witty repartee developed collectively over a few pints of the black stuff!

Given the two types of floor in which interruptions take place, it seems pointless to use a simple quantitative measure to compare men's and women's propensity to interrupt. Counting interruptions cannot tell us how they function or how they are received. I personally remain unconvinced that women interrupt men as often as they are interrupted by them even though I recognize that people's individual and ethnic styles differ and that these styles will interact with gender. Research has shown that among intimate couples (gay and straight) one partner identified as more powerful in terms of decision-making interrupted the other more frequently

(Kollock, Blumstein and Schwartz 1985, cited in James and Clarke 1993). Typically, in heterosexual relations, the male is more powerful. More research along the lines recommended by Ahrens (1997) might clarify definitions and improve methodology.

Politeness

One feature of speech, associated with women since Lakoff (1975) is politeness. Politeness, it is said, can be shown in a variety of ways: intonation; the use of tag questions; attention to hearers' face needs (Brown and Levinson 1978); employment of formulaic politeness particles; choice of mood in verb forms (high use of questions by women, greater use of statements and directives by men); and compliment and apology behaviour (Holmes 1995).

Language expresses a variety of functions, informative, aesthetic, ideological, political, social and affective. We can use language to do different things: a lecturer tends to focus on the informative function when speaking; a parent telling a bed-time story is not just sharing the informative content of the fairy-tale, but also using voice pitch, speed and intonation to amuse, quieten or reassure the child. Similarly, politeness features and strategies are aimed at social and affective cohesion. Politeness has been viewed as part of 'female register' because women are said to be more concerned than men with relationship building and maintenance. According to research by Maltz and Borker (1982), and Goodwin and Goodwin (1987), politeness figures in girls' speech from a very young age and develops as a result of socialization into what amounts to a female sub-culture based on equality, cooperativeness and intimacy. Boys, and later men, on the other hand, are socialized into a sub-culture which values autonomy, hierarchy and competition. As politeness is largely other-oriented, concerned with relationship maintenance and face needs (Brown and Levinson 1978), boys and men, according to this dual cultures perspective, do not develop expertise in accomplishing it. Dominance theorists would, of course, argue that they benefit from it: as social superiors to women, men's positive and negative face needs are constantly being attended to by women.

The terms positive and negative face refer to people's need to be liked and admired and need not to be imposed upon. Politeness operates to soften any potential threat to the hearer's 'face'.

Consider which of the following you would find more acceptable from a neighbour at 10.30 pm:

1. Give me some milk. I've run out.
2. I'm terribly sorry to bother you, but I've run out of milk and my parents have just arrived home from Canada. Could you possibly spare me half a pint till tomorrow?

The first example used a bald directive and a simple reason. The second makes a request using a question and softens the question by using 'could' rather than 'can' and by adding 'possibly'. The request is framed by an initial apology, which is absent from the first. According to Goodwin and other researchers, boys are more likely to use direct commands and girls mitigated commands. Indeed, boys couple commands with assertions of position: aggravated directives. Explanations range from child-rearing patterns, biology, psychological development, socialization and active and deliberate copying of behaviour modelled by adults. Dominance theorists note that differences in style reflect the power hierarchy of society and that all subordinate groups will tend to be more polite than their hierarchical superiors (Deuchar 1989).

Cross-cultural studies have tended to confirm results of research on English, although in some languages, like Japanese, there are gender exclusive particles used by women to signal politeness, formality and deference. In English, any differences in usage are only differences of degree, but there is a wide variety of features associated with politeness. At the phonological level, it has been suggested that a high rising terminal can function as a positive politeness device. Research in New Zealand suggests that women use slightly more of these intonations than men (Britain 1992: 90, cited by Holmes 1995: 104). At the lexical level, we have pragmatic particles such as *I think, you know* and tags, already discussed earlier, as well as choice of register. Standard terms will be viewed as more polite than slang, considered by many writers to be quintessentially male language, along with swearing and cursing. We have already seen that women, especially younger women and working-class women, are not averse to using taboo language. It may carry covert prestige and signal refusal of conventional norms of femininity. Euphemism, similarly, has been considered women's linguistic prerogative (Jespersen 1964 [1922], Lakoff 1975).

No linguistic form has only one meaning. Although modal verb forms like 'could' and 'would' can be used to convey a message politely as in 'would you mind closing the window?' compared to 'shut the window', such verbs can be used less politely:

'Would it kill you to shut the bloody window?'

The same is true in reverse. It can be argued that among a group of young male teenagers constant cursing and swearing can be used to express solidarity – a positive politeness strategy.

Once again, it is crucial to recognize that gender interacts with other social variables such as age, class, regional or ethnic identity and the perceived social distance between speakers. Politeness is not what a person has, as a feature of her personality. Politeness is a set of linguistic (and kinemic) competencies, performed by speakers to accomplish certain interactional needs and goals, within the constraints of cultural norms and expectations. The relationship with the other speaker is central to the degree of politeness used. According to Wolfson (1988), the most significant variable is social distance. We are least likely to be polite with complete strangers and with very close friends and family; it is with casual friends and acquaintances that face needs have to be most appropriately met. She thus proposes a 'bulge' model of politeness which suggests that with this intermediary group between intimates and strangers we actively 'do' politeness: greeting more profusely, apologizing more conscientiously and complimenting more frequently. In a sense, we do not need to be polite to loved ones, nor to strangers, as these relationships are unambiguous. Speakers do know exactly how to address others in normal circumstances, and can feel uncomfortable if someone speaks too familiarly to us. In such cases, we can step up the politeness formulae to re-establish social distance.

A study of politeness in Japanese (Ide *et al.* 1986) challenged the simplistic hypothesis that women are more polite than men and showed that context, pattern of interaction, speaker-addressee distance and occupational status were better predictors than gender of women's polite forms. Another Japanese study (Smith 1992) examined how professional women in Japan could deal with the clash between prevailing gender-based norms of politeness and their superior hierarchical position which required authoritative speech. She found that women did not adopt male directive forms but distinctly female forms of directives, such as those used by mothers to children. Clearly, this would be inappropriate in English, but it does show how no linguistic form is restricted to a single function. Contextual clues, shared knowledge and cultural norms allow hearers to interpret intentions. Thus, in Java, while women are more polite in private contexts, men are expected to be polite in public settings as public politeness connotes power and control (Smith-Hefner 1988).

How are people perceived when they are being polite? Baroni and D'Urso devised an ingenious matched guise experiment which asked subjects to judge one female and one male speaker's recorded telephone request. Using actors, they presented each voice under two separate conditions, one without politeness markers and one with politeness markers added in. Their results showed that adding in politeness markers to the male voice reduces judges' perceptions of the speaker's occupational status and likeableness. The least well-judged voice was that of the polite male. This result reinforces findings which suggest that when women style shift towards masculine norms, they may be disliked (Crawford 1995, Cameron 1995). Baroni and D'Urso (1984) show that being polite is not stigmatizing for a female speaker but can be for a man. Judges considered both the male and female non-polite speakers to be financially better off and in professional employment. This lends credence to the view that it is the less powerful who need to be polite. Power and dominance, rather than sub-cultural norms, seem once again to account more compellingly for gender differences at discourse level.

Summary

- early work in sociolinguistics ignored women or had a male-as-norm bias, against which women's language was viewed as deficient

- dominance-approach linguists argue that men use language to dominate women, while difference-approach linguists argue that two separate but equal gendered styles of interaction exist as a result of early childhood interaction in same-sex peer groups

- postmodernist linguists challenge gender polarity, arguing that speakers enact identities by their linguistic choices and other signalling behaviours such as dress, posture and gesture

- the postmodernist challenge argues that our gender performance constitutes our gender, rather than being a mere instantiation of it

- research on sex-differences in language use has often been contradictory and inconclusive, leading to improvements in design and more nuanced interpretative frameworks

- research highlights how other factors, such as social class, age, ethnic identity and purpose of interaction cut across gender, making it difficult to prove any causal effect in speech patterns

Further reading

Holmes, Janet 1995 *Women, men and politeness*, Longman, London.

Coates, Jennifer 1998 *Language and gender: a reader*, Blackwell, Oxford.

James, Deborah 1996 'Women, men and prestige speech forms: a critical review', in Bergvall, V. *et al.* (eds) *Rethinking language and gender research*, Addison Wesley Longman, New York.

Coates, Jennifer 1993 *Women, men and language* (2nd edition), Longman, Harlow, Part 2, Chapters 4, 5 and 6.

Chapter 7

The dual cultures approach

Chapter outline

This chapter will focus on the popularization of the subcultural perspective. It will:

- explore the positions of those who argue that men and women inhabit different 'worlds'
- produce a critique of this 'dual cultures' model
- investigate and explain the commercial success of works from this perspective
- show why the model has enjoyed more success in the USA than in Europe

Three quite separate positions have emerged from the research outlined in Chapter 6. On the one hand, we have a body of work which consistently argues that differences between men's and women's interactional styles needs to be analysed in terms of women's social subordination. For this group of researchers, difference equals power and inequality. This approach has been called the dominance approach. On the other, we have a body of work which views differences between men and women in interaction as the result of cultural difference. Each sex, it is argued, has its own 'style', each is valid, but miscommunication can result. A third position, associated with postmodernist thinking, argues that individuals may pick and choose among a range of available styles identified as masculine and feminine, and thus perform gender or enact a more or less gender-typed identity. This chapter deals with the second of these approaches, the difference model or dual cultures perspective.

Origins

The dual cultures perspective began as an exploration of the social and linguistic interaction of socially distant groups. Finding that speech act theory (Austin, Searle) failed to account for interaction between different ethnic groups, each of which had intragroup norms at variance with the norms of the other, Gumperz (1982) developed an interactional model which emphasized the dynamic nature of communication in such ethnically mixed encounters. In increasingly multicultural and bureaucratic societies such as those of most Western nations, communication skills have become increasingly important, yet Gumperz shows how ethnic minorities can fare badly in such communities due to a clash of communication styles between non-native speakers and bureaucrats of the dominant majority culture. Gumperz argued that successful interaction or talk requires that individuals share quite subtle strategies for organizing and interpreting utterances in a communicative encounter. The dominant social group tends to 'read' miscommunication as the fault of the ethnic minority speaker and thus develops a stereotyped image of the group as deficient communicators. It is important to note here, given what emerged later, that Gumperz clearly identifies the power dimension in this miscommunication model. The dominant ethnic group does not suffer from the unsuccessful encounter; the minority group does, both symbolically and possibly materially, in terms of unsuccessful negotiation of rights and entitlements, although Gumperz's approach tends to assume good will.

Gumperz's interactional sociolinguistics framework was taken up by Ruth Borker and Daniel Maltz and applied to talk between women and men. Just as different ethnic groups develop intragroup style norms, Maltz and Borker (1982) argue that girls and boys also learn to use language in different ways and that these conversational norms remain into adulthood, leading to distinctive female and male interactional styles.

The dual cultures approach outlined

Noting that girls and boys play in sex-segregated groups at the period when language skills are being developed (five to fifteen), they argue that each sex learns to do different things through

language. According to the dual cultures model, girls learn to create and maintain relationships, criticize others in ways which are
acceptable (be indirect), and interpret the speech of their female
playmates accurately and sensitively. Boys, on the other hand, learn
to assert their position in the group, draw the attention of the other
boys and keep an audience, and assert themselves when another
has the group's attention.

As we have seen, in Chapter 6, these differing skills do correspond to stereotypes associated with women's and men's speech
patterns. For example, in speech, creating and maintaining relationships can be achieved by topic choice, supportive tags, feedback, asking questions, complimenting, eye-contact and close body
positioning, all features associated with female–female talk. Asserting one's dominance, on the other hand, can be achieved by interruption, topic rejection, monologues, failure to ask questions,
silence, lack of feedback and so on. These are features associated
with males in mixed talking encounters.

According to the best-known writers working in this perspective
(Maltz and Borker 1982, Tannen 1990, Goodwin 1995a, Sheldon
1987, 1993), children's playing activities shape world views in
such a way that women's language is one of intimacy, connection
and 'rapport', while men's is one of autonomy, status and 'report'.
According to Tannen, women engage in rapport talk and men in
report talk, two separate genderlects. While rapport talk is associated with the private domain and focuses on building and maintaining intimacy, connection and relationship, report talk tends
to be task oriented, involving giving of information, proposing
solutions to problems and attempting to establish status.

The key point to note about the approach is its argument that
no one is to blame. Women and men are different, talk differently
and miscommunication is inevitable. The solution lies in understanding the problem, accepting the other's difference and aiming for greater flexibility in style. These solutions can, it appears,
be taught, judging by the enormous popular literature which has
emerged in the USA addressed to those who wish to overcome
what Tannen, an otherwise respected linguist, refers to as 'cross-
cultural communication' problems between women and men in
her book *You Just Don't Understand*. This book, and John Gray's
Men are from Mars, women are from Venus, were both 1990s best-
sellers and, although ostensibly addressed to both women and men,
were largely bought by heterosexual women searching for solutions
to very real problems of communication. Tannen also adapted her

prescriptions to women to the workplace situation in her 1995 book *Talking from 9–5* since, as she states in the preface 'clashing conversational styles can wreak havoc at the conference table as well as at the breakfast table' (1995a: 17). Whereas the assertiveness training of the 1980s focused on women as deficient communicators in need of lessons to be more effective, Tannen's work has the merit of recognizing the positive aspects of women's style as understood, and is thus largely non-judgmental.

> Although each style is valid on its own terms, misunderstandings arise because the styles are different. Taking a cross-cultural approach to male–female conversations makes it possible to explain why dissatisfactions are justified without accusing anyone of being wrong or crazy.
>
> (1990: 47)

Critique of the dual cultures approach

One of the first things which strikes the feminist reader of such books is the need to explain their popularity. John Gray's *Men are from Mars, women are from Venus*, and Tannen's *You Just Don't Understand*, have sold over a million copies and topped best-seller lists. Gray has run workshops which, he claims, twenty-five thousand people have attended. Both Tannen and Gray claim that people have told them that reading their book 'saved my marriage'. What is the appeal of such books? Why do these books sell well in the USA and much less elsewhere?

Tannen's and Gray's portrayal of women's and men's conversational styles derives from thirty years of feminist and mainstream research conducted largely from a sex-difference perspective. With the same data, most European feminist sociolinguists have developed an interpretation characterized as a dominance approach. This approach views gender as something constructed, taught and enacted in interaction. Dual cultures models, on the other hand, downplay power completely and tend to view gender as a fixed or essential identity and communication problems as a result of our essential 'styles'. This tendency to downplay negative social forces such as oppression, power and domination has also been noted in other disciplines. Ray Holland, a social psychologist writing in the late 1970s, argued that such 'positive generality' could be put down to unconscious cultural assumptions about the self:

> My most general thesis . . . is that American personality theorists, whilst feeding on ideas from other cultures, notably Europe, persistently misread, misunderstand and finally abuse these ideas. They do it unconsciously so as to make the idea fit their own basic cultural assumptions which emphasize optimistic, self-reliant, healthy, religious (but not obsessively so) individualism.
>
> (1977: 14–15)

Although rejecting the generalization this statement makes, I would argue that the best-seller status of the self-help genre and the publishers' blurb on such books as Gray's and Tannen's can be explained by a belief that current heterosexual arrangements are healthy and that we are in charge of our own lives. These books reflect what Holland called optimism, self-reliance and healthy individualism. Power, alienation and oppression are absent from Gray's and Tannen's representations of marriage, and explicitly so. In response to a stinging review from Troemel–Ploetz (1991) who criticized Tannen's evacuation of the entire issue of inequality between the sexes, Tannen claimed to be talking only about 'quotidian conversational frustrations' (1992: 252) as if power and inequality were not features of such relationships. Crawford (1995: 105) notes on this naïveté:

> It is as though the social structures that award greater power and influence to males exist on another plane (or another planet) and do not intrude into personal relationships. But this is patently false. The structural inequalities of gender *are* reproduced in individual relationships. Thirty years of social science research has shown that men have more power in heterosexual marriage and dating relationships . . .

An obvious consequence of failing to problematize men's greater power, status and access to resources in such popular works is a naïve model of relationship and interaction. As I pointed out earlier with regard to ethnic minorities faced with dominant majority bureaucrats, the effects of miscommunication are not the same for men and women, powerful and powerless participants. Conversation does not just reflect the already existing social inequality between women and men; it can be an instance of it. Style differences cannot be labelled neutral, inevitable or natural, as Gray and Tannen tend to do: they can be a form of 'doing gender' and in male-dominated society 'doing gender' for men means 'doing power over women'.

Even if women and men take on board the suggestions made by these writers (understand, be flexible, try out the other style), it is unlikely that women and men will be treated with the same reactions. Men who eschew the stereotypical male pattern of conversation, become good and attentive listeners and develop relationships through talk may well receive 'brownie points' from their female partners. However, as Crawford shows in her evaluation of assertiveness training for women, trainees who attempt to alter their behaviour towards male norms can be negatively judged, especially by older men (1995: 68). Given that in our society, older men have more power than (younger) women, especially in the workplace, it would appear that adopting cross-gender norms is not the panacea these self-help books claim it to be.

For Gray, heterosexual relationships seem to be based on keeping score of who owes what to whom. He advises men in Chapter 10, 'Scoring points with the opposite sex' that 'there are a variety of ways a man can score points with his partner without having to do much' (1993: 179). Even for committed heterosexuals, such an accountancy approach to marriage must seem distasteful, and to those suffering from serious marital difficulties, facile and inappropriate in its triviality. Tannen, in fairness, does present a more serious case, and is certainly less prescriptive, in keeping with trends in contemporary linguistics.

It would be useful here to examine in detail one of her examples of marital miscommunication. The anecdote I have chosen is one singled out by Tannen's most vociferous critic, Troemel-Ploetz.

Box 7.1 Miscommunication

Tannen outlines the conversation between a woman and one of her women friends following breast surgery. She expresses her distress at the scar tissue and resulting change in contour of her breast. Her friend empathizes and adds that she herself had felt similar distress after similar surgery. When the woman broaches the same topic with her husband, he follows with 'You can have plastic surgery to cover up the scar and restore the shape of your breast' (1990: 49).

The following conversation ensues:

> Woman: 'I'm not having any more surgery! I'm sorry you
>   don't like the way it looks.'
> Man: 'I don't care. It doesn't bother me at all.'

> Woman: 'Then why are you telling me to have plastic
> surgery?'
> Man: 'Because you were saying *you* were upset about the
> way it looked.'

Tannen's comment on this dialogue emphasizes the different conversational needs and strategies of the couple: 'Eve wanted the gift of understanding, but Mark gave her the gift of advice. He was taking the role of problem-solver, whereas she simply wanted confirmation of her feelings' (1990: 50). Troemel-Ploetz notes that in this exchange, the man gets his needs met: men like 'report talk', to give information and advice and to solve problems. The woman, on the other hand, does not get what she needs, validation of her distress, sympathy and reassurance. Tannen argues that men just don't understand what women need. Troemel-Ploetz disputes this:

> Many men, however, must appreciate Tannen's analysis –
> they do not have to find out what women want and, above
> all, they do not have to change. My thesis is that men
> understand quite well what women want but they give only
> when it suits them. In many situations they refuse to give and
> *women cannot make them give.*
>
> (1991: 495)

She goes on to argue that there are structural reasons for this which go well beyond communication style:

> The majority of relationships between women and men in
> our society are fundamentally asymmetrical to the advantage
> of men. If they were not, we would not need a women's
> liberation movement, women's commissions, houses for
> battered women, legislation for equal opportunity,
> antidiscrimination laws, family therapy, couple therapy,
> divorce.
>
> (1991: 495–6)

Troemel-Ploetz also points out that while Tannen 'explains away' men's insensitivity, many men have themselves supported women's attempts, in professional arenas such as the law courts, to identify and eradicate discriminatory verbal behaviours.

> (1991: 499)

Tannen and Gray's failure to attribute any blame to men or to question women's almost constant accommodation to their partner's needs, can be explained by the reference to childhood relationships with peers. If the behaviour of adult women and men can be attributed to patterns developed by children (of their own free will it would seem), then this allows dual cultures theorists not to locate any responsibility with the adults in their day-to-day interactions. The origins of different styles are benign: children cannot be blamed for their conversational habits in the playground. Dating such differences to early childhood reinforces the naïve model of the self. It is as if we become bigger versions of our childhood selves and do not change very much. Once a girl, always a woman. In fact, as Crawford shows, deliberately changing styles to cross-talk is punished for women. They are deemed less likeable and, in some cases, even less competent, when they adopt men's styles, as we have seen. In other words, learned prescriptions on how we are meant to talk maintain inequality and help to enforce people's conformity to gender expectations.

It is equally naïve to suggest that children's same sex peer activity is totally voluntary. The dual cultures approach cannot show why such segregation occurs, fails to notice how it is encouraged by adults, cannot explain (and does not even ask) why certain interactional norms are associated with girls and others with boys. Even if we argue that once children learn which sex they are, they attempt to become as girl-like or as boy-like as possible, this approach cannot explain how or why girls endeavour to develop an identity which is, after all, a stigmatized one.

We need to remember that adults do not interact, speak or play with female and male children the same way. Children are not all allocated the same space (physical or conversational) and this depends on gender. Both mothers and fathers interrupt girl children more than boys (Greif 1980). Children are given different playthings which, in themselves, determine the kind of play which will ensue and the kind of language needed for that play. Clothing and footwear permit or restrict mobility and girls are often required to keep clean and look pretty, requirements which can restrict their activities to sedate, indoor occupations where they have greater contact with adults, adult conversation and domestic routines. Of course, beside these relatively unconscious controls, girls are told to behave and speak in a 'ladylike' manner while boys' use of taboo language may well be more easily indulged: 'boys will be boys'. To argue then that children opt for same-sex play is to miss the subtle coercion that goes on.

Notwithstanding such coercion, girls and boys have ample opportunities to interact together and to watch mixed adult interaction:

in families, school, in television programmes, in the shops, at leisure centres and at the cinema. It is just untenable to suggest that conversational styles develop in same-sex groupings. Gender is often most salient in mixed-sex contexts, where people exaggerate difference to appear to embody a prototypical woman or man. This is particularly true of teenagers, although recent research shows that often teenage girls and boys will both enact some other form of identity, such as straight A athletic or 'burnout' identity (Eckert and McConnell-Ginet 1995). Such research shows that to try to hang differences in communication style upon the single category of sex (especially viewed as an essential attribute of the person, rather than the result of social construction) is to ignore agency as well as to downplay power structures and effects of situation. To argue furthermore that such different styles are equally valid denies that in a male-dominated society, men's style is the positively evaluated style, and it is up to women to accommodate them. In Pamela Fishman's words, women do the 'shitwork' in conversation (Fishman 1983). If men's style were not the prized one in our culture, then we would see courses in 'passivity training' or 'listenership skills' for men, rather than assertiveness training or personal development courses for women.

The final criticism feminists have levelled at the mis-communication self-help genre has been methodological. Although based on serious academic scholarship (which, as we have seen, is in any case inconclusive), these works are anything but scholarly. Findings are rarely attributed to any source, data concerning 'most' women, or 'most' men are presented as 'fact'. Tannen (1990) for example, uses headlines which use present tense relational verbs to suggest the truth of her assertions, as in 'Male–Female Conversation is Cross-Cultural Communication' (my emphasis). Of course, the popular genre requires such language and no doubt, Tannen had to sacrifice more tentative language for a snappy, more sellable style.

The most worrying aspect of this dual cultures approach is the way that it has been used to 'explain' sexual harassment and rape, especially 'date rape'. Young men accused of raping women on a date have been successfully arguing that they 'misunderstood' the woman's signals, and the dual cultures model has been invoked by campus disciplinary committees faced with charges against male students (Crawford 1995: 123). Crawford also cites work on courses in prevention strategies recommended to female students, which shows that young women are made responsible for rape prevention by a focus on their language and communication style in the dating situation. One good student learned her lesson well.

> [W]hat I got out of the whole program was that date rape happens a lot because there is a communication gap between two people . . . I can help protect myself by being more aggressive, giving firm answers, clear signals, and by communicating with the male.
>
> (Corcoran 1992: 135, cited in Crawford 1995: 124)

This notion is not that far from the old 'victim precipitation' view that blames women for their dress, the hours they keep or their alcohol consumption. Now it is our 'signals' that are to blame.

The most positive aspect of the dual cultures approach is that women's style is not systematically categorized as ineffectual or deficient. Earlier applications of sex difference in language research were those of the various schools of assertiveness-training and personal development courses for women. Although such courses did not result directly from language research, such research was used to reinforce the message that in order to be taken seriously women needed to alter their communication style. The dual cultures model has, to a large extent, replaced the plain difference model which underlies the assertiveness movement, and generalizations about women's and men's styles are widely aired in corporate courses aimed at women in middle-management. Instead of being encouraged to adopt the male style, women are now told they may choose, and even that women's more caring and co-operative styles actually make women into better managers. However, so far, such reversals of attitudes towards women's conversational competence have not yet radically altered the gender division of labour. Women still earn 65–70 per cent of men's earnings and the glass-ceiling is still an obstacle to women in both the private and public sectors. Changing our language, it seems, will not change the world.

Summary

- the difference or dual cultures approach argues that women and men form two linguistic sub-cultures, resulting in miscommunication

- the success of popularizations of academic work from this perspective can be explained by the fact that such work fails to challenge power structures in society and makes social problems seem amenable to individual solutions

- the effects of miscommunication are not the same for women and men, nor are the results of trying out the style associated with the other gender

- a worrying result of the acceptance by society of a miscommunication model is the use of its central idea to explain rape and sexual harassment: women are now blamed for not sending clear signals to rapists who 'misunderstand' them

Further reading

Tannen, Deborah 1990 *You just don't understand*, Ballantine, New York.

Troemel-Ploetz, Senta 1991 'Selling the apolitical: (review of Deborah Tannen's *You just don't understand*)', in *Discourse and Society*, 2, 4: 489–502.

Crawford, Mary 1995 *Talking difference: on gender and language*, Sage, London, Chapter 4: 'Two sexes, two cultures'.

Uchida, Aki 1992 'When "difference" is "dominance"; a critique of the "anti-power based" cultural approach to sex differences', in *Language in Society*, 21, 4: 547–68.

Chapter 8

Conclusion: Changing language, changing the world?

Chapter outline

This chapter concludes the book. Its aims are

- to summarize the arguments of Parts 1 and 2
- to examine the language of humour
- to relate feminist work in linguistics to feminist activism in general
- to suggest directions for further work

The arguments

Although Whorfianism is generally discredited within linguistics, we have seen how, in its weaker form, it enjoys support from mainstream and many feminist quarters. Mühlhäusler and Harré (1990), for example, regard pronoun configurations as a reflection of social relations, and feminists such as Bodine (1975), Spender (1985), Schultz (1990) and Silveira (1980) consider that language reflects and reinforces society's male dominance. Implicitly, language reformers, such as feminists and PC advocates, must consider that changing language will change society by changing our thought patterns. Other feminists, such as Cameron (1985, 1995) and Black and Coward (1990) sound a note of caution. Cameron (1995) in *Verbal hygiene* argues that feminist linguists, in proposing language reform, are breaking with linguistics' tradition of describing language and now prescribe usage. Prescriptivism can be criticized on two counts: it is élitist and it does not work. Meyers's (1993) work on *they* as a pronoun in competition with the pseudogeneric *he* prescribed by grammarians shows clearly that despite their pre-scriptions and the support of publishers, teachers and writers, *they* is still widely used by all classes in almost all text-types as well as in spoken language.

A comparison with other languages has shown us that sexism does not reside in language as a result of its gender-marking system. Whether a language is gender-free, has natural gender or grammatical gender, sexist meanings can be inscribed in it. Thus, many feminists argue that we need to change the world and the language will follow. Others, however, consider that language reform has at least the merit of calling into question the assumptions underlying specific linguistic forms. Although coinages like *Ms* have been co-opted and diluted, speakers are now aware that their speech does involve making choices between new forms and traditional ones. In doing so, they mark their affiliations and beliefs. Even if we cannot show that changing language changes social reality, the research on language and perception is consistent and conclusive: using *he or she* rather than *he* does bring women into the mental picture of speaker–hearers, as we saw in Chapter 3.

Feminist speakers of grammatical gender languages like French and German have argued for increased feminization, while English speakers promote neutralization. Feminized forms in English, with specific morphemes like *-ess* or *-ette* connote not only gender but are pejorative in many cases. Thus, what is appropriate for one language may not suit another. Moreover, we need to ask where do we go next, as English speakers, if words which are generic, like *people, citizens and business executives* are construed by speakers and writers as meaning men? The German feminist proposal to feminize and split generics has the merit of constantly signalling female referents in every instance where a general meaning is required. Such splitting is more difficult in some languages than in others, and widely resisted where similar inclusions need to be made in all agreeing parts of speech: articles, adjectives and participles for example.

It appears that the adult male enjoys the status of the prototypical human being; women and children are somehow viewed as not fully human or certainly as not fully autonomous and unique individuals. The almost systematic placing of women in second rank in conjoined phrasing of typical English collocations reminds us of that: Adam and Eve, man and wife, brothers and sisters, Anthony and Cleopatra, Troilus and Cressida, Tristan and Isolde, boys and girls, men and women. Frank and Anshen point out that to get to come first, women need to tote a gun (Frankie and Johnny, Bonnie and Clyde) or hang out with dwarfs (Snow White) (1983: 9). Even *he or she* places women in second place, a reason given for some feminists to use generic *she.*

Why women should always be placed in second position (or not at all) can only be accounted for by feminist theory; it is too systematic to be an accident, arbitrary or coincidental. The feminist theories which best account for the denigration and marginalization of women are, to my mind, those which are open to see analogies between the treatment of women and the treatment of other oppressed groups. Such theories also relate material factors (economic exploitation) to symbolic violence. Writers such as Mies (1986) Shiva (1988), Merchant (1982), French (1986) and Mies and Shiva (1993) provide an analysis which links all such forms of subordination without essentializing women and men. According to such theorists, patriarchal thought is based on sets of interlocking and embedded binary oppositions (woman–man, nature–culture, wild–tamed, black–white, body–mind, subsistence–surplus). These oppositions exist in a hierarchical arrangement: patriarchal cultures give precedence to men, culture, mind and surplus over women, nature, body and subsistence. Moreover, the negative terms – woman, body, nature, wild, emotion – tend to cluster, so that womankind comes to represent all that is negated in the polarization. Collocations reflect these associations: Mother Earth, Earth mother, Mother nature, natural childbirth, natural mother. The gender division of labour reflects the link up between women and nature: women are omnipresent in all spheres where human beings most reveal their animal nature: food preparation, cleaning, nursing, care of the young and elderly, care of the dying. Conversely, men predominate wherever culture overcomes and dominates nature: science, technology, architecture, engineering, mechanics and art.

The polarization is present in stereotypes about women's and men's use of language. Folklinguistic belief has it that women's tongues are out of control. Men are the 'strong, silent' type. Think of the likely terms referring to humans which collocate most easily with *chatter, gossip, tittle-tattle* and *nag.* These stereotypes are the modern equivalent of the scold's bridle, a contraption designed to silence women with opinions unacceptable to men.

Feminist language reform proposals have often been resisted by ridicule. Humour appears harmless yet only works because the hearer of a joke shares the assumptions about the world which the joke depends upon. While racist jokes, such as the Irish joke, are now considered unacceptable in most quarters, misogynistic humour remains rife.

Box 8.1 Misogynistic and feminist humour

A recent anonymous posting to the Internet outlined '100 reasons why it's great to be a guy'. Feminists with a knack for reading 'against the grain' countered the objections of others who found it offensive. A spate of anti-male jokes followed. The content of these jokes shows just how keenly their inventors understand the preoccupations of many heterosexual men. While sexist jokes of the Essex girl/dumb blonde variety work by portraying women as lobotomized nymphomaniacs, the 'male-bashing' jokes posted to the Web challenge the male sexual stereotype beneath all pornography, that of the ever ready predator:

Q: 'Why did Adam come first?'
A: 'Men always do.'
Q: 'Why are men like popcorn?'
A: 'They satisfy you, but only for a little while.'
Q: 'Why do women fake orgasm?'
A: 'Because men fake foreplay.'
Q: 'What do birthdays, toilets and clitorises have in common?'
A: 'Men always miss them.'

Clearly, men's nymphomaniac jokes express their own fear about not being a sexual match for women, and women's jokes about men make private knowledge about specific men, public and generalized. To argue that women's anti-male humour constitutes 'reverse sexism' is to miss the point, however. Feminist humour is a form of resistance. Men's sexist jokes operate in a culture where men also control women by violence, actual and symbolic: prostitution, rape, pornography, trafficking in girls and women, child sexual abuse. This backdrop makes anti-woman jokes more sinister than funny. The poster of '100 reasons why it's great to be a guy', received at my workplace in February 1998, thought apparently that the following were funny:

1. Phone conversations are over in 30 seconds flat
2. Movie nudity is virtually always female
(. . .)
12. Your ass is never a factor in job interviews
(. . .)
22. You can kill your own food
(. . .)
27. You never have to clean the toilet
(. . .)

60. The world is your urinal
(. . .)
64. One mood, all the time!
(. . .)
69. Same work . . . more pay!
(. . .)
99. Baywatch

The vast majority of these 'great reasons for being a guy' are actually great reasons for not being a woman in a patriarchal culture. Reading them against the grain is difficult when they correspond to material practices: sexual exploitation, harassment, unequal job opportunities and the failure of men in heterosexual relationships to do their fair share of housework. When women are taxed with lacking a sense of humour, it usually means we do not laugh at sexist jokes. Male readers are invited to test their own sense of humour on these:

Q: 'Why do midwives slap babies' bottoms when they're born?'
A: 'To knock the penises off the clever ones.'
Q: 'Why is psychoanalysis quicker for men?'
A: 'When it's time to go back to childhood, they're already there.'
Q: 'What's the difference between a woman at 40 and a man at 40?'
A: 'The woman thinks about having children. The man thinks of dating them.'
Q: 'Why are all dumb-blonde jokes one-liners?'
A: 'So men can remember them.'

If world knowledge is necessary to 'get' a joke, it is clear to see why sexist humour is so common and why women have a tough time as comedians. To be seen to be funny, they often have to laugh at other women or deride themselves. A contemporary British comedian, Jo Brand, manages to mix jokes about menstruation, heterosexual sex, men and women, with self-deprecatory comments about her own ample charms. Humorous language, like any language, depends upon context for understanding. In jokes, the context is our entire culture's figuring of women's roles, men's roles, sexuality and power, relationships between different ethnic groups and so on. Women do not tell jokes about fathers-in-law, or mothers-in-law, men tell jokes about mothers-in-law. We can conclude that women's mothers compete with their sons-in-law for loyalty, influence and affection.

Humour, like other forms of verbal interaction, relies on context for its interpretation. Part II of this book has shown that feminists often differ in their interpretations of linguistic data. The interpretations, and the research design itself, depend upon the observers' views and conceptualization of gender. I have argued that gender differences are constructed, and thus made a case against the difference approach in feminist linguistics which sees women's cultural norms as something to be celebrated. It is difficult to celebrate the very norms which are used to constitute us as different and therefore unequal. The problems with the difference approach are many. Women are viewed as a homogeneous group; ethnic differences in style are ignored or denied; the possibility of speaking against the norm is rarely entertained; the underlying view of gender identity is one of relative fixity; other determining factors such as age, class, purpose and setting of interaction, are downplayed; overlap is subordinated and differences exaggerated. Some of these difficulties have arisen because of the limitations of the research context itself. Most studies of 'women's language' have been studies of white middle-class women because most of the researchers have been white middle-class women. Most have been studies of English speakers in Judeo-Christian societies.

During the course of writing, I have been struck by the relative triviality of much of the subject matter I have read. Work in the difference or dual cultures approach in particular seems to evacuate from its analyses any reference to power or violence in women's relationships with men. Dominance perspectives can tend to portray us as victims in their focus on men's power over women. In postmodernist writing resistance seems to focus on ludic gender-bending or gender-blending strategies. For feminists to study language may appear a luxury given the many life-threatening practices which women face world-wide: sexual slavery, profound fundamentalist misogyny, battery, rape, genital mutilation and womanslaughter.

We need to relate patterning in language to patterning in the wider society. We need to change that society in radical ways; reforming language is a useful but woefully inadequate way to do it. However, given the centrality of language to all areas of human endeavour, and its tendency to reflect social arrangements quite precisely, then a study of language can contribute to an interdisciplinary research effort focused on identifying mechanisms of power and violence – physical and symbolic – and structures of inequality. A research focus on resistance rather than victimization may help to shift feminist linguistics away from its current preoccupations and allow the discipline to make a greater, more telling contribution to women's global struggle for human rights.

Summary

- whether a language has no gender-marking, grammatical gender or natural gender, sexist meanings may be inscribed in it

- language reform is more likely to follow than to precede social change in favour of equality

- language reform has the merit of raising awareness about the power of language to marginalize and insult social groups

- there is no language reform which can suit all languages: native speaker intuition about the connotations of linguistic forms will tend to determine proposals for change

- the interpretations and research design of feminist linguists depend upon their underlying conceptualizations of gender and its function in society

- differences in approach within the discipline of sociolinguistics contribute to healthy ongoing debate

- further work needs to be carried out which relates patterning in language to power structures in society, and which focuses on resistance rather than victimization

Further reading

DeFrancisco, Victoria 1997 'Gender, power and practice: or, putting your money (and your research) where your mouth is,' in Wodak, Ruth (ed.) *Gender and discourse*, Sage, London, pp. 37–56.

Mies, Maria 1986 *Patriarchy and accumulation on a world scale*, Zed Books, London.

Shiva Vandana 1988 *Staying alive: women, ecology and development*, Zed Books, London.

References

Abu-Haidar, Farida 1989 'Are Iraqi women more prestige conscious than men? Sex differentiation in Baghdadi Arabic', *Language in Society*, 18: 471–81.

Adams, Carol J. 1996 *The politics of meat*, Continuum, New York.

Aitchison, Jean 1992 *Teach yourself linguistics*, Teach Yourself Books, London.

Ahrens, Ulrike 1997 'The interplay between interruptions and preference organization in conversation: new perspectives on a classic topic of gender research', in Kotthoff, Helga and Wodak, Ruth (eds) *Communicating gender in context*, John Benjamins, Amsterdam, pp. 79–106.

Ainsworth-Vaughn, Nancy 1992 'Topic transitions in physician–patient interviews', *Language in Society*, 21: 409–26.

Andersson, Lars-Gunnar and Trudgill, Peter 1992 *Bad language*, Penguin, Harmondsworth.

Arditti, Rita, D., Klein Renate and Minden, Shelley (eds) 1984 *Test-tube women: what future for motherhood?*, Pandora Press, London.

Aries, Elizabeth 1987 'Gender and communication', in Shaver, Phillip and Hendrick, Clyde (eds) *Sex and gender*, Sage, Newbury Park.

Aries, Elizabeth 1996 *Men and women in interaction: reconsidering the differences*, Oxford University Press, New York.

Aries, Elizabeth 1997 'Women and men talking: are they worlds apart?', in Walsh, Mary Roth (ed.) *Women, men and gender: ongoing debates*, Yale University Press, New Haven.

Arliss, Laurie P. 1990 *Gender communication*, Prentice Hall, New Jersey.

Baron, Dennis 1986 *Grammar and gender*, Yale University Press, New Haven.

Baroni, Maria Rosa and D'Urso, Valentina 1984 'Some experimental findings about the question of politeness and women's speech (Research note)', *Language in Society*, 13: 67–72.

Barrett, Michèle 1988 *Women's oppression today*, Verso, London and New York.

Bass, Ellen and Davis, Laura 1990 *The courage to heal: a guide for women survivors of child sexual abuse*, Cedar, London.

Bem, Sandra L. and Bem, D.J. 1973 'Does sex-biased job advertising "aid and abet" sex discrimination?', *Journal of Applied Social Psychology*, 3: 6–18.

Bergvall, V., Bing, J. and Freed, A. (eds) 1996 *Rethinking language and gender research*, Addison Wesley Longman, New York.

Berlin, B. and Kay, P. 1969 *Basic color terms: their universality and evolution*, University of California Press, Berkeley.

Bing, Janet M. and Bergvall, Victoria L. 1996 'The question of questions: beyond binary thinking', in Bergvall, V. *et al.* (eds) *Rethinking language and gender research*, Addison Wesley Longman, New York.

Black, Maria and Coward, Rosalind 1990 'Linguistic, social and sexual relations: a review of Dale Spender's Man-made language', in Cameron Deborah (ed.) *The feminist critique of language: a reader*, Routledge, London and New York.

Blaubergs, Maija S. 1980 'An analysis of classic arguments against changing sexist language', in Kramarae, Cheris (ed.) *The voices and words of women and men*, Pergamon, Oxford, pp. 135–47.

Bodine, Ann 1975 'Androcentrism in prescriptive grammar: singular *they*, sex-indefinite *he*, and *he or she*', *Language in Society*, 4: 129–46.

Bolinger, Dwight 1980 *Language, the loaded weapon: the use and abuse of language today*, Longman, New York and Harlow.

Bradley, John 1998 'Yanyuwa: "Men speak one way, women speak another"', in Coates Jennifer (ed.) *Language and gender: a reader*, Blackwell, Oxford, pp. 13–20.

Braun, Frederike 1997 'Making men out of people. The MAN principle in translating genderless forms', in Kotthoff, Helga and Wodak, Ruth (eds) *Communicating gender in context*, John Benjamins, Amsterdam.

Britain, David 1992 'Linguistic change in intonation: the use of high rising terminals in New Zealand English', *Language Variation and Change*, 4: 77–104.

Brouwer, Dédé and Van Hout, Roeland 1992 'Gender-related variation in Amsterdam vernacular', *International Journal of the Sociology of Language*, 94: 99–122.

Brown, Penelope and Levinson, Stephen 1978 'Universals in language usage', in Goody, Esther N. (ed.) *Questions and politeness: strategies in social interaction*, Cambridge University Press, Cambridge, pp. 56–310.

Brown, Roger and Gilman, Albert 1960 'The pronouns of power and solidarity', in Sebeok, Thomas A. (ed.) *Style in language*, MIT Press, Cambridge MA, pp. 253–76.

Bucholtz, Mary *et al.* (eds) 1994 'Cultural performances' Proceedings of the third Berkeley Women and Language conference.

Burgen, Stephen 1996 *Your mother's tongue: a book of European invective*, Victor Gollancz, London.

Butler, Judith 1990 *Feminism and the subversion of identity*, Routledge, London and New York.

Cameron, Deborah 1985 *Feminism and linguistic theory*, Macmillan, London.

Cameron, Deborah (ed.) 1990 *The feminist critique of language*, Routledge, London and New York.

Cameron, Deborah 1992a 'Naming of parts: gender, culture and terms for the penis among American college students', *American Speech*, 67, 4: 367–82.

Cameron, Deborah 1992b 'Not gender difference but the difference gender makes – explanation in research on sex and language', *International Journal of the Sociology of Language*, 94: 13–26.

Cameron, Deborah 1995 *Verbal hygiene*, Routledge, London and New York.

Cameron, Deborah and Coates, Jennifer 1989 'Some problems in the sociolinguistic explanation of sex differences', in Coates, Jennifer and Cameron, Deborah (eds) *Women in their speech communities*, Longman, New York, pp. 13–26.

Cameron, Deborah *et al.* (eds) 1992 *Researching language: issues of power and method*, Routledge, London.

Cannon, Garland and Roberson, Susan 1995 'Sexism in present-day English – is it diminishing?', *Word* 36, 1: 23–35.

Carreiras, Manuel *et al.* 1996 'The use of stereotypical gender information in constructing a mental model: evidence from English and Spanish', *The Quarterly Journal of Experimental Psychology*, 49, 3: 639–63.

Cherry, Kittredge 1991 *Womansword: what Japanese words say about women*, Kodansha International, Tokyo.

Cheshire, Jenny 1982 'Linguistic variation and social function', in Romaine Suzanne (ed.) *Sociolinguistic variation in speech communities*, Edward Arnold, London, pp. 153–6.

Cheshire, Jenny and Trudgill, Peter (eds) 1998 *The sociolinguistics reader*, vol. II *Gender and discourse*, Edward Arnold, London.

Chesler, Phyllis 1990 *Sacred bond: motherhood under siege*, Virago, London.

Chilton, Paul A. 1988 *Orwellian language and the media*, Pluto, London.

Clark, Kate 1992 ' "The linguistics of blame": representations of women in *The Sun*'s reporting of crimes of sexual violence', in Toolan, Michael (ed.) *Language, text and context. Essays in stylistics*, Routledge, London and New York, pp. 208–26.

Coates, Jennifer 1989 'Gossip revisited: Language in all-female groups', in Coates, Jennifer and Cameron, Deborah (eds) *Women in their speech communities*, Longman, London and New York, pp. 94–122.

Coates, Jennifer 1993 *Women, men and language* (2nd edition), Longman, Harlow.

Coates, Jennifer 1996 *Women talk: conversation between women friends*, Blackwell, Oxford.

Coates, Jennifer 1998 *Language and gender: a reader*, Blackwell, Oxford.

Coates, Jennifer and Cameron, Deborah (eds) 1989 *Women in their speech communities*, Longman, London and New York.

Corbett, Greville 1991 *Gender*, Cambridge University Press, Cambridge.

Corcoran, C. 1992 'From victim control to social change: a feminist perspective on campus rape prevention programs', in Chrisler, J. and Howard, D. (eds) *New directions in feminist psychology*, Springer, New York, pp. 130–40.

Corea, Gena 1988 *The Mother Machine*, The Women's Press, London.
Crawford, Mary 1995 *Talking difference: on gender and language*, Sage, London.
Daly, Mary 1978 *Gyn/Ecology: the metaethics of radical feminism*, Beacon Press, Boston.
DeFrancisco, Victoria Leto 1991 'The sounds of silence: how men silence women in marital relations', *Discourse and Society*, 2, 4: 413–23.
DeFrancisco, Victoria Leto 1997 'Gender, power and practice: or putting your money (and your research) where your mouth is', in Wodak Ruth (ed.) *Gender and discourse*, Sage, London, 37–56.
De Klerk, Vivian 1992 'How taboo are taboo words for girls?', *Language in Society*, 21: 277–89.
Delphy, Christine 1984 *Close to home: a materialist analysis of women's oppression*, translated and edited by Diana Leonard, London, Hutchinson.
Delphy, Christine and Leonard, Diana 1992 *Familiar exploitation: a new analysis of marriage in contemporary western societies*, Polity, Oxford.
Deuchar, Margaret 1988 'A pragmatic account of women's use of standard speech', in Coates, Jennifer and Cameron, Deborah (eds) *Women in their speech communities*, Longman, London and New York, pp. 27–32.
Dhaouadi, Mahmoud 1996 'Un essai de théorisation sur le penchant vers l'accent parisien chez la femme tunisienne', *International Journal of the Sociology of Language*, 122: 107–25.
Dixon, R.M.W. 1972 *The Dyirbal language of North Queensland*, Cambridge University Press, Cambridge.
Duchen, Claire 1986 *Feminism in France: from May 1968 to Mitterrand*, Routledge, London.
Duchen, Claire (ed.) 1987 *French connections: voices from the women's movement in France*, Hutchinson, London.
Eagly, Alice H. 1997 'Comparing women and men: methods, findings and politics', in Walsh, Mary Roth (ed.) *Women, men and gender: ongoing debates*, Yale University Press, New Haven, pp. 24–31.
Eckert, Penelope 1989 'The whole woman: sex and gender differences in variation', *Language Variation and Change*, 1: 245–68.
Eckert, Penelope and McConnell-Ginet, Sally 1995 'Constructing meaning, constructing selves: snapshots of language, gender and class from Belten High', in Hall, Kira and Bucholtz, Mary (eds) *Gender articulated: language and the socially-constructed self*, Routledge, London, pp. 469–507.
Edelsky, Carol 1981 'Who's got the floor?', *Language in Society*, 10, 3: 383–421.
Edwards, Betty 1979 *Drawing on the right side of the brain*, J.P. Tarcher, Los Angeles.
Ehrlich, Susan and King, Ruth 1994 'Feminist meanings and the (de) politicization of the lexicon', *Language in Society*, 23: 59–76.
Eisikovits, Edina 1987 'Sex differences in inter-group and intra-group interactions among adolescents', in Pauwels Anne (ed.) *Women and language in Australian and New Zealand society*, Australian Professional Publications, Sydney, pp. 45–58.

Elgin, Suzette Haden 1985 *Native Tongue*, Women's Press, London.

Fairclough, Norman 1992 *Discourse and social change*, Polity Press, Cambridge.

Fausto-Sterling, Anne 1985 *Myths of gender: biological theories about women and men*, Basic Books, New York.

Firth, J.R. 1935 'The technique of semantics', in *Transactions of the Philological Society*, reprinted in Firth, J.R. 1959 *Papers in linguistics 1934–1951*, Oxford University Press, London.

Fishman, Pamela 1983 'Interaction: the work women do', in Thorne, B., Kramarae, C. and Henley, N. (eds) *Language, gender and society*, Newbury House, Rowley, MA, pp. 89–102.

Frank, Francine and Anshen, Frank 1983 *Language and the sexes*, State University of New York Press, Albany.

Freed, Alice F. 1994 'A cross-cultural analysis of language and gender', in Bucholtz, Mary *et al.* (eds) *Cultural Performances*, Proceedings of the third Berkeley Women and Language conference, pp. 197–204.

Freed, Alice F. and Greenwood, A. 1996 'Women, men, and type of talk: what makes the difference?', *Language in Society*, 25: 1–26.

French, Marilyn 1986 *Beyond Power: on women, men and morals*, Ballantine Books, New York.

Fromm, Erich 1972 'The Erich Fromm theory of aggression', *New York Times Magazine*, 27 February.

Gal, Susan 1979 *Language shift: social determinants of linguistic change in bilingual Austria*, Academic Press, New York.

Garcia-Guadilla, N. 1981 *Libération des femmes: Le MLF*, Presses Universitaires de France, Paris.

Geary, James 1997 'Speaking in tongues', *Time*, July 7, pp. 52–8.

Gershuny, H. Lee 1973 'Sexist semantics: An investigation of masculine and feminine nouns and pronouns in dictionary sentences that illustrate word-usage as a reflection of sex-role', University of New York Ph.D dissertation.

Gibbon, Margaret 1993 'Ethnic subnationalism: cultural factors in its emergence and development', in Böck, R. and Kelly, M. (eds) *France: Nation and Regions*, University of Southampton.

Gibbon, Margaret 1995 'Sex and the translator', in *Working papers in language and society*, Dublin City University.

Gibbon, Margaret 1996 'The discourses of infertility treatment: A French–English comparison', in Hickey, T. and Williams, J. (eds) *Language, education and society in a changing world*, Multilingual Matters, Clevedon, pp. 170–8.

Giles, Howard and Powesland, P. 1975 *Speech style and social evaluation*, Academic Press, London.

Gilligan, Carol 1982 *In a different voice: psychological theory and women's development*, Harvard University Press, Cambridge, MA and London.

Goldsmith, Andrea E. 1980 'Notes on the tyranny of language usage', in Kramarae, Cheris 1980 *Voices and words of women and men*, Pergamon, Oxford, pp. 179–91.

Goodwin, Marjorie H. and Goodwin, Charles 1987 'Children's arguing', in Philips, S., Steele, S. and Tanz, C. (eds) *Language, gender and sex in comparative perspective*, Cambridge University Press, Cambridge, pp. 200–48.

Gordon, Elizabeth 1994 'Sex differences in language: another explanation?', *American Speech*, 69, 2: 215–21.

Gouëffic, Louise 1996 *Breaking the patriarchal code: the linguistic basis of sexual bias*, Knowledge, Ideas and Trends Inc., Manchester CT.

Gourvès-Hayward, Alison 1998 'Color my world', in Singelis, Theodore M. (ed.) *Teaching about culture, ethnicity and diversity: exercises and planned activities*, Sage, Thousand Oaks and London, pp. 207–13.

Graddol, David and Swann, Joan 1989 *Gender voices*, Blackwell, Oxford.

Gray, John 1993 *Men are from Mars, Women are from Venus*, Thorsons, London.

Greif, E. 1980 'Sex differences in parent–child conversations', in Kramarae Cheris (ed.) *The voices and words of women and men*, Pergamon, Oxford pp. 253–8.

Grice, Paul 1957 'Meaning', *Philosophical Review*, 66: 377–88.

Grice, Paul 1975 'Logic and conversation', in Cole, Peter and Morgan, Jerry L. (eds) *Speech acts* vol. III of *Syntax and semantics*, Academic Press, New York.

Griffin, Susan 1978 *Woman and nature: the roaring inside her*, Harper and Row, New York.

Guillaumin, Colette 1987 'The question of difference', in Duchen Claire (ed.) *French connections: voices from the women's movement in France*, Hutchinson, London, pp. 64–77.

Gumperz, J. (ed.) 1982 *Language and social identity*, Cambridge University Press, Cambridge.

Hall, Kira and Bucholtz, Mary (eds) 1995 *Gender Articulated: Language and the socially-constructed self*, Routledge, London.

Hall, Kira and O'Donovan, Veronica 1996 'Shifting gender positions among Hindi-speaking hijras', in Bergvall, V.L., Bing, J.M. and Freed, A.F. (eds) *Rethinking language and gender research: theory and practice*, Addison Wesley Longman, New York.

Halliday, Michael A.K. and Hasan, Ruqaiya 1989 *Language, context and text: aspects of language in a social-semiotic perspective*, Oxford University Press, Oxford.

Hamilton, Edith and Cairns, Huntingdon 1963 *Plato: the collected dialogues*, Princeton University Press, Princeton NJ.

Hardman, M.J. 1996 'The sexist circuits of English', *The Humanist*, 56, 2: 25–32.

Hartmann, Heidi 1981 'The unhappy marriage of Marxism and feminism: towards a more progressive union', in *The unhappy marriage of Marxism and feminism: a debate on class and patriarchy*, edited by Lydia Sargent, Pluto Press, London.

Hellinger, Marlis 1980 'For men must work and women must weep. Sexism in English language textbooks used in German schools', *Women's Studies International Quarterly*, 3: 267–75.

Henle, P. (ed.) 1958 *Language, thought, and culture*, University of Michigan Press, Ann Arbor.

Henley, Nancy 1977 *Body politics: Power, sex and non-verbal communication*, Prentice Hall, New Jersey.

Herring, S., Johnson, Deborah A. and Di Benedetto, T. 1995 'This discussion is going too far! Male resistance to female participation on the Internet', in Hall, Kira and Bucholtz, Mary (eds) *Gender articulated: Language and the socially constructed self*, Routledge, London, pp. 67–96.

Herriot 1970 *Introduction to the psychology of language*, Methuen, London.

Holland, Ray 1977 *Self and social context*, Macmillan, London.

Holmes, Janet 1986 'Functions of you *know* in women's and men's speech', *Language in Society*, 15: 1–22.

Holmes, Janet 1995 *Women, men and politeness*, Longman, London.

Holmes, Janet 1997 'Women, language and identity', *Journal of Sociolinguistics*, 1, 2: 195–223.

Houston, Marsha and Kramarae, Cheris 1991 'Speaking from silence: methods of silencing and of resistance', *Discourse and Society* (special issue on women and language), pp. 387–99.

Hughes, Susan E. 1992 'Expletives of lower working-class women', *Language in Society*, 21: 291–303.

Hymes, Dell 1972 'On communicative competence', in Pride, J.B. and Holmes, J. (eds) *Sociolinguistics*, Penguin, Harmondsworth, pp. 269–93.

Ide, Sachiko *et al.* 1986 'Sex difference and politeness in Japanese', *International Journal of the Sociology of Language*, 58: 25–36.

Irigaray, Luce 1977 *Ce sexe qui n'en est pas un*, Editions de Minuit, Paris.

Irigaray, Luce 1985 *This sex which is not one*, edited by C. Porter, Cornell University Press, New York.

James, Deborah 1996 'Women, men and prestige speech forms: a critical review', in Bergvall, V., Bing, J. and Freed, A. (eds) *Rethinking language and gender research*, Addison Wesley Longman, New York, pp. 98–125.

James, Deborah and Clarke, Sandra 1993 'Women, men and interruptions: a critical review', in Tannen, Deborah (ed.) *Gender and conversational interaction*, Oxford University Press, Oxford, pp. 231–80.

James, Deborah and Drakich, Janice 1993 'Understanding gender differences in amount of talk: a critical review of research', in Deborah, Tannen (ed.) *Gender and conversational interaction*, Oxford University Press, Oxford, pp. 281–312.

Jaworski, Adam 1989 'On gender and sex in Polish', *International Journal of the Sociology of Language*, 78: 83–92.

Jespersen, Otto 1894 *Progress in language*, Macmillan, New York.

Jespersen, Otto 1964 *Language: its nature, development and origin*, W.W. Norton & Co. Inc. [Henry Holt & Co., Inc., 1922] New York.

Kalbfleisch, Pamela J. and Cody, Michael J. (eds) 1995 *Gender, power and communication in human relationships*, Lawrence Erlbaum Associates Inc., New Jersey.

Kay, Paul and Kempton, Willet 1984 'What is the Sapir–Whorf hypothesis?', *American Anthropologist*, 86, 1: 65–79.

Keenan, Elinor 1974 'Norm-makers, norm-breakers: uses of speech by men and women in a Malagasy community', in Bauman, Richard and Sherzer, Joel (eds) *Explorations in the ethnography of speaking*, Cambridge University Press, Cambridge, pp. 125–43.

Key, Mary Richie 1996 *Male/female language*, University of California, Irvine.

Khosroshahi, Fatemeh 1989 'Penguins don't care, but women do: A social identity analysis of Whorfian problem', *Language in Society*, 18: 505–25.

Kiesling, Scott Fabius 1998 'Men's identities and sociolinguistic variation: The case of fraternity men', *Journal of Sociolinguistics*, 2, 1: 69–99.

Kim, Min-Sun and Bresnahan, Mary 1996 'Cognitive basis of gender communication: a cross-cultural investigation of perceived constraints in requesting', *Communication Quarterly*, 44, 1: 53–70.

Kipers, Pamela S. 1987 'Gender and topic', *Language in Society*, 16: 543–57.

Kocourek, Rostislav 1982 *La langue française de la technique et de la science*, Brandstetter, Wiesbaden.

Kollock, P., Blumstein, P. and Schwartz, P. 1985 'Sex and Power in interaction', *American Sociological Review*, 50: 34–46.

Konishi, Toshi 1994 'The connotations of gender: a semantic differential study of German and Spanish', *Word*, 45, 3: 317–27.

Kotthoff, Helga and Wodak, Ruth (eds) 1997 *Communicating gender*, John Benjamins, Amsterdam.

Kramarae, Cheris (ed.) 1980 *The voices and words of women and men*, Pergamon Press, Oxford.

Kramarae, Cheris and Treichler, Paula A. 1985 *A feminist dictionary*, Pandora Press, London.

Kramsch, Claire 1993 *Context and culture in language teaching*, Oxford University Press, New York.

Kress, Gunther and Hodge, Robert 1979 *Language as ideology*, Routledge and Kegan Paul, London, Boston and Henley.

Kurzon, Dennis 1989 'Sexist and nonsexist language in legal texts: the state of the art', *International Journal of the Sociology of Language*, 80: 99–113.

Labov, William 1969 *The study of nonstandard English*, National Council of Teachers of English, Urbana, Illinois.

Labov, William 1966 *The social stratification of English in New York City*, Centre for Applied Linguistics, Washington.

Labov, William 1972 *Sociolinguistic patterns*, University of Pennsylvania Press, Philadelphia.

Labov, William 1991 'The intersection of sex and social class in the course of linguistic change', *Language Variation and Change*, 2: 205–54.

Lakoff, George 1987 *Women, fire and dangerous things: what categories reveal about the mind*, University of Chicago Press, Chicago.

Lakoff, George and Johnson, M. 1980 *Metaphors we live by*, University of Chicago Press, Chicago.

Lakoff, Robin 1975 *Language and woman's place*, Harper and Row, New York.

Langford, Wendy 1997 'Bunnikins, I love you snugly in your warren: voices from subterranean cultures of love', in Harvey, Keith and Shalom, Celia *Encoding sex, romance and intimacy*, Routledge, London, pp. 170–85.

Larkin, Joan 1975 'Vagina sonnet', *Amazon Quarterly*, 3, 2: 59.

Leclerc, Annie 1974 *Parole de Femme*, Grasset, Paris.

Lee, David 1992 *Competing Discourses: perspective and ideology in language*, Longman, London.

Leech, Geoffrey N. 1981 *Semantics* (2nd edition), Penguin, Harmondsworth.

Lieberson, Stanley 1984 'What's in a name? . . . some sociolinguistic possibilities', *International Journal of the Sociology of Language*, 45: 77–87.

Livia, Anna and Hall, Kira (eds) 1997 *Queerly phrased: language, gender and sexuality*, Oxford University Press, Oxford and New York.

Lynch, C.M. and Staussnoll M. 1987 'Mauve washers: sex differences in freshman writing', *English Journal*, 76: 90–4.

Macaulay, Monica and Brice, Colleen 1994 'Gentlemen prefer blondes: a study of gender bias in example sentences', in Bucholtz, Mary *et al.* (eds) *Cultural Performances*, Proceedings of the third Berkeley Women and Language conference, pp. 449–61.

Macaulay, Monica and Brice, Colleen 1997 'Don't touch my projectile: gender bias and stereotyping in syntactic examples', *Language*, 73, 4: 798–825.

Maccoby, E.E. and Jacklin, C.N. 1974 *The Psychology of sex differences*, Stanford University Press, Stanford.

MacKay, Donald G. 1983 'Prescriptive grammar and the pronoun problem', in Thorne, B., Kramarae, C. and Henley, N. *Language, Gender and Society*, Newbury House, Rowley, MA, pp. 33–53.

Maltz, Daniel and Borker, Ruth 1982 'A cultural approach to male–female miscommunication', in Gumperz, J. (ed.) *Language and social identity*, Cambridge University Press, Cambridge.

Mandelbaum, David (ed.) 1949 *Selected writings of Edward Sapir*, University of California Press, Berkeley.

Marks, Elaine and De Courtivron, Isabelle (eds) 1981 *New French feminisms: an anthology*, Harvester, Brighton.

Martyna, Wendy 1980 'The psychology of the generic masculine', in McConnell-Ginet, S., Borker, R. and Furman, N. (eds) *Women and Language in literature and society*, Praeger, New York.

McConnell, Allen R. and Fazio, Russell H. 1996 'Women and men as people: effects of gender-marked language', *Personality and Social Psychology Bulletin*, 22, 10: 1004–13.

McConnell, Allen R. and Gavanski, I. 1994 'Women as men and people: occupational title suffixes as primes', paper presented at the 66th Annual Meeting of the Midwestern Psychological Association, Chicago, May 1994.

McConnell-Ginet, Sally 1979 'Prototypes, pronouns and persons', in Mathiot, Madeleine (ed.) *Ethnolinguistics: Boas, Sapir and Whorf revisited*, Mouton, The Hague.

McConnell-Ginet, Sally 1989 'The sexual (re)production of meaning', in Frank, Francine and Treichler, Paula (eds) *Language, gender and professional writing*, Modern Languages Association, New York.

McConnell-Ginet, S., Borker, R. and Furman, N. (eds) 1980 *Women and language in literature and society*, Praeger, New York.

McElhinny, Bonnie 1998 'I don't smile much any more: affect, gender and the discourse of Pittsburgh police officers', in Coates, Jennifer 1998 *Language and gender: a reader*, Blackwell, Oxford.

McKeon, Richard (ed.) 1968 *The basic works of Aristotle*, Random House, New York.

Merchant, Carolyn 1982 *The death of nature: women, ecology and the scientific revolution*, Wildwood House, London.

Meyers, M.W. 1993 'Forms of *they* with singular noun phrase antecedents: evidence from current educated English usage', *Word*, 44, 2: 181–92.

Miemitz, Bärbel 1997 ' "Male person" vs "Everything that is not a male person". Gender and sex in Polish', in Kotthoff, Helga and Wodak, Ruth (eds) *Communicating gender in context,* John Benjamins, Amsterdam, pp. 31–50.

Mies, Maria 1986 *Patriarchy and accumulation on a world scale*, Zed books, London.

Mies, Maria and Shiva, Vandana 1993 *Ecofeminism*, Fernwood Publications, London.

Miller, Casey and Swift, Kate 1976 *Words and women: new language in new times*, Anchor/Doubleday, New York.

Mills, Sara 1992 'Knowing your place: a Marxist feminist stylistic analysis', in Toolan, Michael (ed.) *Language, text and context: essays in stylistics*, Routledge, London and New York, pp. 182–205.

Mills, Sara 1995 *Feminist stylistics*, Routledge, London.

Milroy, Lesley 1980 *Language and social networks*, Blackwell, Oxford.

Milroy, Lesley 1992 'New perspectives in the analysis of sex differentiation in language', in Bolton, Kingsley and Kwok, Helen (eds) *Sociolinguistics today: international perspectives*, Routledge, London and New York, pp. 163–79.

Milroy, Lesley and Milroy, James 1992 'Social network and social class: Toward an integrated sociolinguistic model', *Language in Society*, 21: 1–27.

Modan, Gabriella 1994 'Pulling apart is coming together: the use and meaning of opposition in the discourse of Jewish-American women', in Bucholtz, Mary *et al. Cultural performances*, Proceedings of the 3rd Berkeley Women and Language conference.

Moi, Toril 1985 *Sexual/textual politics*, Methuen, London.

Morris, Meaghan 1982 'A-mazing Grace: notes on Mary Daly's poetics', *Intervention*, 16: 70–92.

Mühlhäusler, P. and Harré, R. 1990 *Pronouns and people: the linguistic construction of social and personal identity*, Blackwell, Oxford.

Nair Rukmini, Bhaya 1992 'Gender, genre and generative grammar: deconstructing the matrimonial column', in Toolan, Michael (ed.) *Language, text and context. Essays in stylistics*, Routledge, London and New York, pp. 227–54.

Nelson, Marie Wilson 1998 'Women's ways: Interactive patterns in predominantly female research teams', in Coates, Jennifer *Language and gender: a reader*, Blackwell, Oxford, pp. 354–72.

Newman, Michael 1992 'Pronominal disagreements: the stubborn problem of singular epicene antecedents', *Language in Society*, pp. 447–75.

Ng, S.H. 1990 'Androcentric coding of *man* and *his* in memory by language users', *Journal of Experimental Social Psychology*, 25: 455–64.

Nichols, Patricia 1983 'Linguistic options and choices for Black women in the rural south', in Thorne, B., Kramarae, C. and Henley, N. *Language, gender and society*, Newbury House, Rowley MA.

Nielsen, Elizabeth 1988 'Linguistic sexism in business writing textbooks', *Journal of Advanced Composition*, 8: 55–65.

Nilsen, A. *et al.* 1977 *Sexism and language*, National Council of Teachers of English, Urbana, Illinois.

Nowaczyk, R.H. 1982 'Sex-related differences in the color lexicon', *Language and Speech*, 25: 257–65.

Oakley, Ann 1972 *Sex, gender and society*, Maurice Temple Smith, London.

O'Barr, William M. and Atkins, Bowman K. 1980 'Women's language or powerless language?', in McConnell-Ginet, Sally *et al.* (eds) *Women and language in literature and society*, Praeger, New York, pp. 93–110.

Omi, Michael and Winant, Howard 1994 *Racial formation in the United States: from the 1960s to the 1990s*, Routledge, New York.

Pateman, Trevor 1982 'MacKay on singular *they* (discussion)', *Language in Society*, 11: 437–8.

Penelope, Julia 1990 *Speaking freely: unlearning the lies of the fathers' tongues*, Pergamon Press, Oxford.

Philips, S., Steele, S. and Tanz, C. (eds) 1987 *Language, gender and sex in comparative perspective*, Cambridge University Press, Cambridge.

Pinker, Steven 1994 *The language instinct*, Penguin, Harmondsworth.

Polanyi, Livia and Strassmann, Diana 1993 'Storytellers and gatekeepers in economics', paper presented to Committee on the Status of Women in Linguistics conference on language and gender, Ohio State University, Columbus.

Poynton, Cate 1989 *Language and gender: making the difference*, Oxford University Press, Oxford.

Raymond, Janice G. 1979 *The transsexual empire*, Women's Press, London.

Raymond, Janice G. 1986 *A passion for friends*, London, The Women's Press.

Reid, Julie 1995 'A study of gender differences in minimal responses', *Journal of Pragmatics*, 24: 489–512.

Reynolds, Katsue Akiba 1998 'Female speakers of Japanese in transition', in Coates, Jennifer *Language and gender: a reader*, Blackwell, Oxford.

Risch, Barbara 1987 'Women's derogatory terms for men: That's right, "dirty" words', *Language in Society*, 16: 353–8.

Romaine, Suzanne 1997 'Gender, grammar, and the space in between', in Kotthoff, Helga and Wodak, Ruth (eds) *Communicating gender in context*, John Benjamins, Amsterdam, pp. 51–76.

Rosch, Eleanor 1975 'The nature of mental codes for color categories', *Journal of Experimental Psychology: Human Perception and Performance*, 1: 303–22.

Rosch Eleanor 1977 'Human categorization', in Warren, Neil (ed.) *Studies in cross-cultural psychology*, Academic Press, London, pp. 1–49.

Rosenblum, Karen E. 1986 'Revelatory or purposive? Making sense of a "female register"', *Semiotica*, 59: 157–70.

Russ, Joanna 1983 *How to suppress a woman's writing*, University of Texas Press, Austin.

Sachs, Albie and Wilson, Joan Hoff 1978 *Sexism and the law: a study of male beliefs and legal bias in Britain and the United States*, Martin Robertson, Oxford.

Sachs, J., Lieberman, P. and Erickson, D. 1973 'Anatomical and cultural determinants of male and female speech', in Shuy, Roger W. and Fasold, Ralph W. (eds) *Language and attitudes: current trends and prospects*, Georgetown University Press, Washington DC, pp. 74–84.

Sacks, H., Schegloff, E. and Jefferson, G. 1974 'A simplest systematics for the organisation of turn-taking in conversation', *Language*, 50, 4: 696–735.

Saeed, John I. 1997 *Semantics*, Blackwell, Oxford.

Sarah, Elizabeth 1980 'Teachers and students in the classroom: an examination of classroom interaction', in Spender, Dale and Sarah, Elizabeth (eds) *Learning to lose: sexism and education*, Women's Press, pp. 155–64.

Schieffelin, Bambi B. 1987 'Do different worlds mean different words?: an example from Papua New Guinea', in Philips, S., Steele, S. and Tanz, C. (eds) *Language, gender and sex in comparative perspective*, Cambridge University Press, Cambridge, pp. 249–60.

Schultz, Muriel R. [1975] 1990 'The semantic derogation of women', in Thorne, Barrie and Henley, Nancy (eds) *Language and sex: difference and dominance*, Newbury House, Rowley, MA, pp. 64–75, reprinted in Cameron, Deborah (ed.) *The feminist critique of language: a reader* Routledge, London, pp. 134–47.

Segal, Lynne 1987 *Is the future female? Troubled thoughts on contemporary feminism*, Virago, London.

Serbin, Lisa A. and O'Leary, Daniel K. 1975 'How nursery schools teach girls to shut up', *Psychology Today*, 20: 57.

Sheldon, Amy 1993 'Pickle fights: gendered talk in preschool disputes', in Tannen, Deborah (ed.) *Gender and conversational interaction*, Oxford University Press, New York.

Sherman, Julia 1983 'Factors predicting girl's and boy's enrollment in college preparatory mathematics', *Psychology of Women Quarterly*, 7: 272–81.

Shiva, Vandana 1988 *Staying alive: Women, ecology and development*, Zed books, London.

Silveira, Jeanette 1980 'Generic masculine words and thinking', in Kramarae, Cheris (ed.) *The voices and words of women and men*, Pergamon, Oxford, pp. 165–78.

Simon, Sherry 1996 *Gender in translation: cultural identity and the politics of transmission*, Routledge, London and New York.

Simpson, J. and Tarrant, A.W.S. 1991 'Sex and age-related differences in colour vocabulary', *Language and Speech*, 34: 57–62.

Smith, Janet S. 1992 'Women in charge: politeness and directives in the speech of Japanese women', *Language in Society*, 21: 59–82.

Smith, P.M. 1985 *Language, the sexes and society*, Oxford, Blackwell.

Smith-Hefner, Nancy J. 1988 'Women and politeness: the Javanese example', *Language in Society*, 17: 535–54.

Spender, Dale 1985 *Man-made language* (2nd edition), Routledge and Kegan Paul, London.

Spretnak, Charlene 1982 *The politics of women's spirituality: essays on the rise of spiritual power*, Garden City, New York, Anchor Books.

Strunk, W. and White, E.B. 1979 *The elements of style* (3rd edition), Macmillan, New York.

Swaringen, S. *et al.* 1978 'Sex differences in colour naming', *Perceptual and Motor Skills*, 47: 440–2.

Tannen, Deborah 1990 *You just don't understand*, Ballantine, New York.

Tannen, Deborah 1992 'Response to Senta Troemel-Ploetz "Selling the apolitical", 1991', *Discourse and Society*, 3: 249–54.

Tannen, Deborah 1995a *Talking from 9 to 5: women and men at work: language, sex and power*, Virago, London.

Tannen, Deborah 1995b *Gender and Discourse*, Oxford University Press, Inc., New York and Oxford.

Tannen, Deborah 1993 (ed.) *Gender and conversational interaction*, Oxford University Press, New York.

Taylor, John G. 1974 *Black holes: the end of the universe?*, Random House Inc., New York.

Thomas, Beth 1989 'Differences of sex and sects: linguistic variation and social networks in a Welsh mining village', in Coates, Jennifer and Cameron, Deborah (eds) *Women in their speech communities*, Longman, New York, pp. 51–60.

Thorne, Barrie and Henley, Nancy (eds) 1975 *Language and sex: difference and dominance*, Newbury House, Rowley, MA.

Toolan, Michael (ed.) 1992 *Language, text and context: essays in stylistics*, Routledge, London.

Troemel-Ploetz, Senta 1991 'Selling the apolitical (review of Deborah Tannen's *You just don't understand*)', *Discourse and Society*, 2, 4: 489–502.

Trudgill, Peter 1972 'Sex, covert prestige and linguistic change in the urban British English of Norwich', *Language in Society*, pp. 179–95.

Uchida, Aki 1992 'When "difference" is "dominance": a critique of the "anti-power-based" cultural approach to sex differences', *Language in Society*, 21: 547–68.

Vendler, Zeno 1977 'Wordless thoughts', in McCormack, William C. and Wurm, Stephen A. (eds) *Language and thought: anthropological issues*, Mouton, The Hague and Paris.

von Flotow, Luise 1997 *Translation and gender: translating in the 'Era of feminism'*, St Jerome, Manchester.

Walsh, Mary Roth (ed.) 1997 *Women, men and gender: on-going debates*, Yale University Press, New Haven.

Walters, Keith 1996 'Gender, identity, and the political economy of language: Anglophone wives in Tunisia', *Language in Society*, 25, 4: 515–55.

West, Candace 1984 *Routine complications: troubles with talk between doctors and patients*, Indiana University Press, Bloomington.

West, Candace 1995 'Women's competence in conversation', *Discourse and Society*, 6, 1: 107–31.

West, Candace [1984] 1998 'When the doctor is a "lady": Power, status and gender in physician–patient encounters', in Coates Jennifer *Language and gender: a reader*, Blackwell, Oxford.

Wetzel, Patricia J. 1988 'Are "powerless" communication strategies the Japanese norm?', *Language in Society*, 17: 555–64.

Whaley, C.R. and Antonelli, George 1983 'The birds and the beasts –
woman as animal', *Maledicta*, 7: 219–29.

Wierzbicka, Anna 1986 'Does language reflect culture? Evidence from
Australian English', *Language in Society*, 15: 349–74.

Wilson, E. and Ng, S.H. 1988 'Sex bias in visual images invoked by
generics: a New Zealand study', *Sex Rules*, 18: 159–69.

Wilson, Fiona 1992 'Language, technology, gender, and power', *Human
relations*, 45, 9: 883–904.

Wodak, Ruth (ed.) 1997 *Gender and discourse*, Sage, London.

Wolfe, Susan 1993 'Reconstructing PIE terms for kinship and
marriage', *Word*, 44, 1: 41–51.

Wolfe, Susan J. and Stanley, Julia P. 1980 'Linguistic problems with
patriarchal reconstructions of Indo-European culture: a little more
than kin, a little less than kind', in Kramarae, Cheris (ed.) *The voices
and words of women and men*, Pergamon, Oxford, pp. 224–37.

Wolfson, Nessa 1988 'The bulge: a theory of speech behaviour and
social distance', in Fine, J. (ed.) *Second language discourse: A textbook of
current research*, Ablex, Norwood NJ, pp. 21–38.

Yang, Yonglin 1996 'Sex and level-related differences in the Chinese
color lexicon', *Word*, 47, 2: 207–20.

Zajonc, R.B. 1962 'Response suppression in perceptual defense', *Journal
of Experimental Psychology*, 64: 206–14.

Zimmerman, Don H. and West, Candace 1975 'Sex roles, interruptions
and silences in conversation', in Thorne, Barrie and Henley, Nancy
(eds) *Language and Sex*, Newbury House, Rowley, MA, pp. 105–29.

Glossary

The definitions given here are, of necessity, simplifications of terms found in the text. Refer to cited sources for further amplification.

accommodation: this occurs when a speaker's language converges towards the speech of the listener. Speakers accommodate to other's speaking styles to secure approval, reduce social distance or to increase comprehension.

active voice: describes the verb form in sentences where the agent (or doer) of the verb is the subject, e.g. 'Jane scored a goal' contrasts with passive voice 'A goal was scored by Jane'.

address: terms or forms of address refer to the ways speakers address listeners. Feminists note that women and men often use unreciprocated terms of address ('Sharon', Mr Brown) and that women are addressed as intimates by strangers ('Love', 'Pet', 'Honey').

adjacency pair: a set of two utterances in the turn-taking model of conversation. The first utterance is the stimulus and the second the response, e.g. invitation–acceptance, greeting–greeting, apology–minimization.

agency: in stylistics, agency refers to who acts and who is acted upon. In feminist theory, especially that influenced by postmodernist thought, agency refers to human ability to act/choose/invent identity.

agent: The subject of an active sentence. In passive sentences, the agent may be unexpressed or deleted, e.g. 'Mary was beaten by her husband' may become 'Mary was beaten'.

agreement: a requirement in certain languages to show the relationship between elements by marking them as similar. In grammatical gender languages, articles and adjectives agree with nouns for number (singular and plural) and for gender.

androcentrism: organizing principle of male-dominated cultures whereby men's viewpoint is naturalized to seem generalizable to all people.

arbitrariness: refers to the unmotivated connection between a concept and the word used to signify it. In Whorfianism, arbitrariness refers to a culture's choice of what to name and what to leave un-named.

articulatory setting: muscular postures we control which affect voice pitch and delivery.

asymmetric setting: a speech situation where speakers are socially unequal, e.g. doctor–patient, magistrate–defendant encounters.

backchannelling: feedback in conversation to signal listener's attention. It may involve sounds and words (mmhm, right, yeah) or non-verbal cues like nodding. Some feminist linguists argue that women use more backchannelling devices than men.

background knowledge: knowledge shared by speaker and listener, or assumed to be shared.

binary oppositions: sets of terms considered to be polar opposites, e.g. black–white, girl–boy.

canon: the texts most highly valued by a society. Feminists and anti-racists have argued that the literary canon is composed of the work of 'DWEMs' – dead white European males.

categorization: the human tendency to classify and organize.

code-switching: occurs when a speaker shifts from using one language to another (in the case of bilingualism) or from one variety to another, such as standard and regional dialects.

collocation: the tendency for certain words to occur with or near other words with higher frequency than chance. 'Sleek' is more likely to be used with 'cat' for example, than with 'dog'.

competence: in Chomskyan linguistics, refers to speakers' underlying knowledge of the rules of their language which allows them to produce an infinite number of correct sentences. Contrasts with performance, which is the actual utterances speakers produce.

connotation: the associations words may have for speakers, beyond the dictionary definition of meaning.

co-operative strategy: conversational behaviour which speakers adopt to ensure participants can all contribute what they wish to interaction. Some feminists argue this characterizes women's conversation.

Contrasts with competitive strategies where speakers use interruption, overlap, silence to control conversational topics and dominate interaction.

covert prestige: in sociolinguistics, an explanation for the tendency of some speakers to prefer non-standard speech forms. Applied especially to working-class men and young women. Contrasts with overt prestige associated with standard or élite language varieties.

critical linguistics: linguistics which draws attention to how political positions are framed in language.

default gender: one of a range of terms to describe the use of the masculine gender in contexts where either or both genders may be understood. See also *generic he*.

denotation: contrasting with connotation, refers to the dictionary meaning of a word. 'Rottweiler' denotes a specific breed of dog but may connote fear, danger and injury to a bitten child, for example.

descriptivism: method and principle underlying contemporary linguistics, which sets out to describe usage, rather than to prescribe it. Contrasts with *prescriptivism*.

determinism: in linguistics, determinism refers to the idea that our language determines perception and thought. See also *linguistic relativity* and *Sapir–Whorf hypothesis*.

dialect: a social or regional variety of language, with identifying features like particular vocabulary items, accent and grammatical structures.

diglossic: said of a community where two different languages or two very different varieties of a language co-exist, one normally being formal (H, or High) and the other informal (L, or Low).

diminutive: said of a form with an added morpheme to connote cuteness, triviality or familiarity, or to denote small size, e.g. kitchenette, Suzie, Barbie.

discourse: in linguistics, refers to an extended written or spoken text which has a structure which helps to define it. In cultural theory, discourse refers to sets of beliefs and statements with some form of patterning or homogeneity, which can be identified or 'unpacked' by close, critical reading.

dispreferred response: an undesired response in an adjacency pair. The preferred response to an invitation is acceptance, the dispreferred response is a refusal. Dispreferred responses may threaten hearer's face. See also *face, face needs*.

dual cultures perspective: also termed sub-cultural model, or difference approach, this position in sociolinguistics argues that women and men have different cultural norms underlying their conversational behaviour.

dyad: a conversational pair.

elicitation: a term used to refer to the method of obtaining linguistic data from informants. Tacit recording, interviewing and reading tests are some of the techniques used to elicit such data.

epicene: a noun which can refer to females or males without changing its form, e.g. 'journalist', 'teacher', 'doctor'. The fact that 'male' is added to 'nurse', shows 'nurse' is not truly epicene. Grammatical gender languages can have epicenes, e.g. French: 'la or le linguiste', 'la or le journaliste'.

essentialism: belief in biological determinism, that is that women and men behave and speak differently and that this is due to different essential natures.

euphemism: a word or phrase used instead of one which is not socially acceptable in a particular context.

face: a term used in pragmatics and sociolinguistics in analyzing politeness in language. Positive and negative face refer to the desire to show connection with others and not to offend them, respectively.

face needs: the need of a speaker to be liked and not to be offended or insulted.

female: adjective referring to biological womanhood, as opposed to feminine, referring to socially constructed behaviour expected of women. See also *grammatical gender.*

feminism: a range of philosophies and theories about women's social position in male-dominated societies, allied to activism, to bring about radical change.

function: as used in this book, the role language plays in a specific context, depending on purposes of the speakers in engaging in conversation, or of writers in the production of texts. A lecture's main function will be to inform, a conversation's may be to express intimacy or to amuse and so on.

gender: a grammatical term used for the classification of nouns, e.g. feminine, masculine or neuter; animate or inanimate. In feminist theory, gender refers to the ways biologically female and male individuals are made into women and men by socialization into roles and behaviours consonant with society's demands.

genderlect: a term coined by feminist linguists to refer to patterning of language usage said to be more common to one gender. For example, men are said to be less polite and to use more non-standard forms than women.

gender-marking: in morphology, the addition of endings or prefixes to denote gender, e.g. sculptor/sculptress. In such pairs, the masculine terms is often the default term, used for generic purposes.

generic: forms used to refer to all members of a class, thus to women and men.

generic masculine (GM) words: forms which refer theoretically to women and men, but which have a male-only meaning also, e.g. 'man' as the species term, as well as the term for an adult male. Feminist language reform proposals target such forms.

generic pronoun: a pronoun which can stand for either female or male referents. Some linguists consider English lacks a true generic pronoun. Feminists challenge prescriptive 'he' as generic and propose alternatives such as 's/he', 'he or she', 'she' or 'they'.

grammatical gender language: one in which all nouns, including inanimates like 'turnip', 'table' and 'book' are gendered. Contrasts with natural gender languages which mark only animates for gender. English, with its she/he/it distinctions, is said to be based on natural gender.

hedge: in pragmatics and conversational analysis, refers to terms and expressions which are hearer-oriented and express tentativeness, evasiveness or approximation, e.g. 'sort of', 'kind of', 'more or less'. Considered by some to be used more by women than men.

hypothesis: an idea which can be tested against empirical proof.

ideal speaker–hearer: in Chomskyan linguistics, an idealized language user who understands and speaks correctly formulated speech, without the communication failure typical of real language.

ideology: a set of beliefs held to be self-evidently correct, even natural, but which are rooted in stereotypes determined by economic, political and social interests.

latching: in the turn-taking model of communication, the perfect situation where a hearer anticipates exactly when a speaker will finish and begins her/his turn at that precise moment, without pause or overlap.

lexical gap: absence of a term in a language to correspond to a concept which may be lexicalized in another. English divides kin by gender (sister–brother, aunt–uncle) but fails to do so for 'cousin', whereas French has two words (cousine, cousin). Some feminists claim that English lacks many words to express meanings and experiences salient to women.

lexicography: the compilation of dictionaries.

lexis: words, the vocabulary of a language.

linguistic determinism: see *determinism.*

linguistic relativity: the idea that our language influences the way we view reality. See also *Sapir–Whorf hypothesis.*

MAN: male-as-norm principle in language, related to idea of best exemplar of a prototype. Revealed in sentences like: 'Lecturers can now avail of sabbatical leave payments which entitle them to bring their wives along for free when they travel abroad.'

man-made language: feminist view of language which considers it has been developed by men to encode males' experiences and views of the world. See *androcentrism.*

markedness: in morphology and semantics, the notion that there are unmarked or base forms of words and derived or inflected marked forms. In most languages, the masculine form is considered unmarked (with generic or default capacity) and the feminine marked, e.g. 'actor/actress'.

masculine: considered appropriate to men. See also *grammatical gender.*

matched-guise experiment: a procedure used in sociolinguistic research to uncover unconscious beliefs and attitudes about language varieties held by informants.

maxims of conversation: also termed Gricean maxims, the principles said to underlie conversation; to be truthful, to say enough but not too much, to make contributions relevant to the exchange, to be clear and unambiguous.

mentalese: the language of thought, as opposed to spoken language.

metalanguage: language about language and expressions which draw attention to language, such 'so to speak', 'so-called', 'strictly speaking'.

metaphor: words and phrases which draw attention to similarity between apparently dissimilar things, events, people. Metaphor is pervasive in language. For example, we describe our moods in terms of the directions up and down: 'he's feeling low', 'I'm on cloud nine', 'she's down in the dumps', 'things are picking up for us', 'we have our ups and downs'. For feminists, metaphors reflect social beliefs about women and men. See *semantic derogation*.

modals: verbs which modify other verbs, such as 'may', 'might', 'must', 'can'. Some conversational analysts argue that women use them to reduce the power of their assertions.

morpheme: the smallest unit of a word which carries meaning. For example, smallest has two: 'small' and '-est', the superlative, and 'stewardess' has two also, with '-ess' being a morpheme signalling female. See *markedness* and *gender-marking*.

native speaker intuition: using the judgements of native speakers of a language for linguistic data collection. Considered unreliable by many linguists, who prefer to collect samples of actual speech.

natural gender language: see *grammatical gender language*.

neutralization: in language reform circles, the strategy of removing gender-marked language and adopting gender-free forms. Contrasts with feminization, a strategy preferred by feminist speakers of grammatical gender languages.

nominalization: making a noun out of a verb or adjective. Like agent deletion, nominalization can obscure responsibility for events, cf. 'The management locked out strikers'/ 'The lock-out began at 8 pm.'

non-standard: see *standard*.

onomastics: the study of names (of people and places).

onomatopoeia: words whose sounds imitate the noise of a physical event or animal signal, e.g. hiss, plop, splash, miaow.

overlap: an interruption occurring within the last syllable of another speaker's turn. See also *transition relevance place*.

overt prestige: prestige attaching to use of standard language, or forms valued by powerful groups and institutions. Contrasts with covert prestige.

passive: see *active voice*.

patriarchy: organization of society according to men's needs and interests, to the detriment of women.

pejoration: a change in the meaning of a word over time whereby it loses positive or neutral connotations and comes to acquire negative overtones. See *semantic derogation of women*.

performance: see *competence.*

politically correct: said of behaviour and of language which aims to be inclusive and avoid offence to minority groups and women.

pragmatic particles: words and phrases like 'kind of', 'sort of', 'you know' and tag questions, all of which contribute to understanding and interaction in conversation.

preferred response: see *dispreferred response.*

prescriptivism: see *descriptivism.*

pronoun: also called proform, a word which substitutes for another to avoid repetition, e.g. Jane came home and then *she* serviced the car. See also *generic pronoun.*

prototype: a typical or best example of a category, e.g. 'apple' or 'orange' for fruit, rather than 'fig', 'date' or 'tomato'. The male-as-norm principle appears to grant men the status of a prototype of a human being.

quotative: a form which introduces direct speech, e.g. 'she said', 'he went', 'like'.

redundant: said of a distinction which does not need to be made. Gender marking in grammatical gender languages is largely redundant.

referent: real-life thing or concept, to which a word refers.

register: a variety of language defined according to characteristics of its users, or of the social context, e.g. scientific English, slang, regional dialect.

repair: occurs in conversation when a speaker attempts to fix some deficiency, e.g. 'sorry, you were saying?'

root: base form of a word, e.g. 'helplessness' has a root 'help' and two affixes, '-less' and '-ness'.

Sapir–Whorf hypothesis: named after Edward Sapir (1884–1939) and Benjamin L. Whorf (1897–1941), a theory about the relationship between language, thought and the perception of reality, which argues that the language we speak influences, or even determines, how we perceive reality. Underlies the views of many feminist linguists who propose language reform.

semantics: within linguistics, the study of meaning.

semantic derogation of women: the tendency for words relating to women to acquire negative overtones. See *pejoration.*

sex: biologically given category, compares with gender, which is socially constructed.

sex-exclusive: said of a language form which is prescribed for one gender, and proscribed for the other.

sex-preferential: said of a language feature found to be used more by one gender than the other. See also *genderlect*.

socialization: the processes by which an individual is conditioned and educated to behave according to norms of her/his culture, including the adoption of gender-appropriate conduct.

sociolinguistics: the study of how social factors (age, gender, class etc.) are reflected in language use.

standard: prestige variety of a language, described in grammar books and taught to non-native learners of the language. Contrasts with non-standard varieties, considered incorrect by prescriptivists. See *covert* and *overt prestige*.

stereotype: belief or set of beliefs, often largely erroneous, about a group of people and their behaviour. Rarely tested against actual individual behaviour, the stereotype operates as a short-cut for thinking or observation.

subject: see *agent*.

syntax: how words combine to form sentences; word order and relationships between elements in the sentence.

taboo: behaviours, language which a society forbids or obscures by attaching a stigma to it. Taboo differs from culture to culture.

tag-question: a minimal verb and pronoun sequence at the end of a statement, e.g. That's nice, *isn't it?* or 'you're not going, *are you?* Tag questions have been said to be used more by women than men by some linguists.

target language: in translation, the language into which a text is translated. Contrasts with source language.

term of address: see *address*.

transcription: written version of spoken language, including symbols to show pauses, interruptions etc.

transition relevance place: obvious point in a speaker's turn when next speaker may begin speaking without violating underlying rules of co-operation in interaction. May be identified by pitch, body language (especially gaze) or linguistic features.

turn-taking: the conversational behaviour of shifting from one speaker to another, as governed by an underlying model of interaction.

turn-taking violation: interruptions and overlaps with previous speaker. See *transition relevance place*.

unmarked: see *markedness* and *gender-marking*.

variable: in sociolinguistics, a form for which a range of alternatives exists, corresponding to stylistic requirements to social context.

variety: a distinct form of language, e.g. a regional or occupational variety of English.

vernacular: local speech variety. In diglossic communities, the variety which carries connotations of in-group loyalty and affiliation.

Whorfianism: see *determinism*, *Sapir–Whorf hypothesis* and *linguistic relativity*.

Index